Dear Cla...
I hope this...
you on your journey forward.

101 Tips for the

Budding Medium

Best wishes

By Chris Page

Chris Page

Front cover and section headings are by the wonderful
Shelley Youell and are subject to copyright

ISBN: 978 0 86071 844 4

A Commissioned Publication Printed by
MOORLEYS
Print, Design & Publishing
info@moorleys.co.uk · www.moorleys.co.uk

Contents

Trust the unusual
Remember spirit can use your life experiences
Don't embellish or interpret
Don't be surprised
Practice, practice, practice
Don't despair
Regularly reassess your goals
Make the most of your meetings
Don't be discouraged
Use the dynamics of your group to move forward
Encourage others
Make a point of seeing other mediums in several venues
Build your library
Try to use numbers
Explore colour when you see it
Grandmothers are special people
Remember that when in the power everything is relevant
Seek out the special item
Expand on the information
Consider if you were the 'dead' person
Before the message
The gift from spirit
Always relay the message
Sometimes nothing is everything
Be aware when you are inspired
Never give up
Try to see your steps
Be an explorer!
Try healing mediumship
Re-set your intention
Feel into healing energies
Be aware of your healing progress
Don't use your own energy
Prepare to be an all-day everyday medium
Set your focus
Maintain your focus too
Don't question your sitter
Be conscious of your approach to spirit
Review your targets
Be easy on yourself
Practice sitting with spirit

About the Author

I was born in Belper, Derbyshire, England in December 1951. My first recollection of spirit[1] was about 8 years later. I was in bed with a heavy cold/flu and in and out of sleep. I woke up once to see quite clearly a Native American standing by my bed who threw an assortment of bones and other small items on the floor. He drifted away, or I dropped back to sleep in probably about a minute. I felt very comfortable with him and had no fear whatsoever. I found out many years later that around that time two of my aunts frequented the local spiritualist church, so maybe they asked for healing for me and a healer decided to visit.

Not too long after this I started having vivid dreams where I would travel out of my body and around the local park and streets. This seemed very natural to me and I presumed that everyone could do it. I found out this was not an ordinary dream when I spotted some relations walking through the park towards my house. I woke myself up and told my parents who was coming, they didn't believe me as there was no reason for them to visit so late in the evening. About two minutes later they turned up at the door to inform us of the passing of another relative.

These dreams continued and I found myself regularly meeting other children in them. We seemed to be in a constant state of play and comfort above the clouds. I remember no discord whatsoever; it was a blissful time. After a couple of visits I found my way there very easily. When these dreams were ending a funnel appeared in the clouds down to my room at home. This was like a helter- skelter and was fun. I believe that the children I played with were mostly in spirit but I can just recollect others having

---

[1] The universal oneness that some call God.

funnels of their own, so I guess they were in the same state as me. It was about twenty years later that I first heard the term astral projection which I investigated and came to the conclusion that that was what I was doing as a child. I believe that I visited what Andrew Jackson Davis called the 'Summerland'. He being one of the great pioneers of the Spiritualist movement.

So, after my childhood experiences things went quiet for a while, school, then an active social, work and sporting life seemed to halt any proceedings in the direction of spirit.

In my late teens I was drawn to books about spirit which I avidly read the whole section in the local library and then on a rare trip to London my eye was caught by a book called 'The third eye', I read it on the journey and although I didn't understand it, not knowing what the third eye was, it reignited my interest, and I take this as a definite piece of guidance to what was to become the largest and most important part of my life(family excepted of course).

It was around this time that I moved jobs as for some reason I could not settle and yet another coincidence occurred when my new office directly overlooked the local Spiritualist church; which again purely by happenstance I had passed each day on my walk to and from school. Looking back there were so many instances where my future was hinted at by my spirit team. Perhaps it is the same for you, my reader, and this type of coincidence is ringing a few bells.

Just a few years later, now married, my wife went to see a psychic[2], and, me being me, I asked her to book me in anonymously so I could expose her as a fraud. There was no apparent way that the

---

[2] A person who is able to connect and read the energies surrounding every individual.

medium[3] could have known what she did and I suspected trickery. In the event she astounded me and I immediately got to wondering how this could be. She had given me information that I had not told anyone and although most of what she told me was psychic, not mediumship it was enough to keep me interested and want to pursue it. Things she told me were still coming true thirty years later. Not knowing who to ask about this I decided to talk to my father who said he knew nothing of it but knew someone who did. This was the start of a period of great change and some amazing events.

The person my father referred me to was a work colleague of his who, again, seemingly by chance lived directly behind me and we could chat over the boundary wall. This gentleman turned out to be a transfiguration[4] medium and he lent be a raft of books to study. These were mainly published by the Psychic Book Club I think or maybe the Psychic Press, I must say that I didn't really take much notice. What really inspired me was that although these books were by many different authors over a large time scale there wasn't a single time that I found a contradiction either within a book or between different books. This seemed very strange as I expected there to be lots of differing views and opinions but they all seemed to fall naturally into place.

This is where my great experiences with the spirit world really began.

The first major thing that happened to me was the day I returned the books. I said how much I had enjoyed reading them all and was invited to join a circle the very next day. I didn't feel that I was

---

[3] A person who is aware of those in spirit and is able to pass on information about them.

[4] A form of mediumship where the face of the medium is moulded to the features of one in spirit, or alternatively, a mask of the person in spirit is made and placed in front of the face of the medium.

ready for this but as I was about to say no my mouth refused to move and the only word I could say was yes. I wasn't frightened by this but it was uncanny having words formed in my mouth I really didn't intend saying. So that was it, I had been invited to my first circle[5]!

The group I had been invited to was a healing group and there were several trance mediums in it. I was to be involved with this group for 25 years and rarely missed a week. In fact, the majority of the time it was twice weekly, and so I was present at around 2000 trance events including the specials. Quite an apprenticeship!

My first experience was beyond any expectations I might have had. I was taken aback at first by the religious aspect of it, and in many ways I feel this is unnecessary but many people are comforted by prayer. So, we started in prayer and sang a hymn and by this stage I was thinking, 'Oh no, I'm in the wrong place'. Then a medium went into trance[6] and within five minutes there I was discussing with his guide about his life and times during the English Civil War! This was at once amazing yet unbelievable, and it was an unusual introduction to the spiritual world. I remember the next day wondering if it was a dream!

Another strange thing happened at the end of that first circle. I was asked if I would like to come for healing on the following Monday and once again, the only word that would form in my mouth was 'yes'. This was what brought about the major change in my life. I had been suffering with severe back pain since childhood which, being stubborn, did not stop me doing what I wanted to do, notably playing rugby, which did nothing to help the situation. In

---

[5] A group of people or an occasion when people meet to communicate with spirit.

[6] A form of mediumship using an altered state of mind which allows the blending of the medium with someone in spirit.

any event, I went to the healing service the following Monday and watched the proceedings until I was asked if I would like to receive healing. I sat on the stool expecting nothing and then when the healers approached I felt enormous energy around me and a feeling of great comfort. Then, as if I was in a shower, starting at the top of my head a wonderful feeling poured through me and washed all of my pain and anxiety away completely. All of my pain had disappeared in just a few minutes. It seemed to just drop into the floor.

On my way home I had lots of questions. Why does no one know of this; why isn't it taught in schools etc. The main question was however, 'Can I learn to do this'. It took two years of attending every week before I was allowed to attempt healing in partnership with a trained healer. Another great leap forward.

So, twenty-five years later having sat in this trance circle I started thinking about other aspects of mediumship. I had had no aspirations to do anything other than heal up till this point. I had enormous admiration and respect for those healers who worked in the trance state but never had any thoughts on working this way myself. This was about to change!

Purely by chance, again, I got talking to an acquaintance in a pub of all places. There was a band playing and I remarked 'Look at that! They are called The Faith Healers! I've been doing that for 30 years! At which his companion said 'really' and we got talking. As I remarked, purely by chance she taught the development group at the local church. She invited me to attend, and I did.

It was in that group that I found that I had had the ability to do most things and this in turn led me to develop into working in trance state, mainly in the area of healing together with working on clairvoyance and mediumship in general. Within a year I was demonstrating under supervision and just about after two years was working[7] at psychic suppers. I had moved to another church by this time and was told my development group teacher not to come again! Why not? You need to go out and do it! Surprise, surprise by the end of the week I had been asked if I took services. I said 'Yes!'

The first service did not go well, I gave three messages to the same person, two to another and a couple of others that were wishy washy at best. It could not have been too bad though as they rebooked me, and I still work at that church to this day.

This was probably the time when the real learning started. There is no real substitute for practice, and my bookings came thick and fast thereafter and I was soon booked every weekend. It was hard to resist and say no. I maybe should have but I didn't.

This is where learning comes in. From the first time I borrowed books from my neighbour I carried on studying about the Who, How, and Why of mediumship which I still do. It is in this pursuit of knowledge that I first attended the Arthur Findlay College on an open day. To say that I was impressed was an understatement. I knew that this was the beginning of a great new chapter in my life.

So, along with learning at home and in circles I attended courses in mediumship and healing and also trained to be an SNU approved healer, (my previous healing being in a private group.)

---

[7] Work or working is the word we use to describe the time we spend whether within a group or when contacting spirit for someone else.

I have attended the AFC[8] on numerous occasions since that first open day and the level of teaching is nothing short of excellent, maybe astounding, and the nature of the college itself seems to help immensely.

I recommend in this book continuation of learning and sitting regularly with spirit, the results can be spectacular on occasion but the general steady progression in the many ways of attuning to spirit is assured.

In recent years my personal development has been in public demonstration and in linking trance with healing. This has led to working with others in a teaching role too, both in the UK and abroad, which came unexpectedly and unlooked for. This seems to be the way of spirit work. Things happen when we least expect and areas that we would not expect to be working in somehow appear in our path.

Finally, I would like to note that everything I have undertaken in spirit work has brought great joy and satisfaction, and hopefully has brought peace, comfort and contentment to those I have worked with.

---

[8] The Arthur Findlay College of Psychic Studies, a world renowned college for those seeking to enhance their mediumship.

Introduction

Why have you opened this book?

Maybe you found that you were just a little different from the norm. Maybe you always knew you were a little different. Perhaps you have seen things most people can't, perhaps too, you knew of forthcoming events; maybe you were passed it by a friend who felt inspired to choose you to pass it on to. Occasionally people just know things, or personalities or any kind of knowledge which seems to spring out of nowhere, and that makes them think that there is 'something else' to life. Many people have hints of what is to come and the time isn't right for it to manifest, others are aware of the spirit world all their lives from an early age and don't mention it because they think it's normal.

Others too are discouraged because their experiences don't fall in line with the doctrine of where they were brought up. Many of our very best mediums in the past had a great struggle with this when minds weren't so open as nowadays.

So, why has this ability fallen on you? Well why not?

Perhaps too, like me, you found there were questions to be answered.

For whatever reason we have decided to journey the path less travelled.

Whatever reason you have for reading this book I hope you enjoy it. Enjoyment is very important in all we do with our work with spirit, if it is not fulfilling and enjoyable then we are usually doing something wrong.

Let's explore some of these events that lead to this path because some, many or lots of the above may ring true with you as an individual.

Many people, if not all, have a discernible level of psychic ability, but because this is natural to them, they don't think anything of it, perhaps it is dismissed as happenstance, although it can manifest in many ways. Lots of those destined to develop this in later years may show actual mediumship, again being unaware of what it is. This is why, as parents, we should encourage children to talk about what they see and hear even if we can't see or hear it ourselves. I remember here talking with my three-year-old son who was talking to someone I couldn't see while sitting at the top of the stairs. When asked what he was doing he said, 'I'm fishing with this gentleman', a gentleman I couldn't see but knew that he could. You may well have had a similar experience either as a child or parent. This is fine and natural, a pointer perhaps of the potential in the child to become something special. At this point I must say that we as mediums are not special but we are at the thin end of the bell-shaped curve of humanity in the respect of communication with those who have trod this path before.

It is quite likely that as a reader of this book, you have experienced unusual things and have certain abilities that don't seem quite normal. This is good! It shows a potential for you to express yourself and the world of spirit and hopefully to act as an ambassador or a spokesperson for those in spirit.

So again, why not you? Where does this 'path less travelled' start? The answer is you are already on it, it has been there since before you were born, it is part of your destiny. Hopefully you are ready to take up this destiny or you are already treading the path wisely, for there are many distractions and many people who would like to stop you in order to pursue their own vision. Try to avoid the distractions, just because you have found, and indeed become part of the pursuit of little-known knowledge does not mean that every product of the vivid imaginations of others is true.

If, for example you have a belief in dragons and unicorns think again. These are wonderful creatures in fantasy fiction but what we are pursuing is truth. Nothing else. And how wondrous it is! Surely enough for anyone.

So, the path less travelled is not easy, with many an incline, but it is straight and solid underfoot for it is grounded on truth. You can go forward at your own pace with confidence. How far you can go depends in great part to your natural inclination but more so to your commitment and your objectives. Aim high, take a look, then set the bar higher. The other thing about the path less travelled is that it has no ending it goes on and on, ever improving.

Don't you think that's wonderful?

Section 1: In the Beginning

'Walk the fields of humanity with a pure heart'
'Ariel,' spirit guide of Arline Doherty, 15 July 2020

Replace fear of the unknown with curiosity

As you set out on this process of investigation and learning about the spirit world and how to communicate with them it is important that you have a pure heart. That your learning is not just for yourself but for everyone you touch. This certainly does not mean that you try to give everyone you meet in the street or the supermarket a message from a loved one, far from it. It means that you try to have a pure heart in your approach to everyone you can with compassion and understanding. As we are all different each and every person you talk to has something to offer. Your actions have an influence on them too so, 'Walk the fields of humanity with a pure heart!'

Early on in the process of your journey into mediumship you will need to set your goals.

If your goals are fame and fortune, think again! The path of the medium is one of service. The wealth it brings is a wealth of inner peace and contentment. It is beyond value.

Your goals may be constantly evolving as you discover you have latent talents in areas you have not thought about. Nevertheless, it is important to signal to your spirit team the ways in which you would like to work, so they can influence you in aligning with your ambitions. So, your current abilities, showing how you are working already and which you need to expand, and the abilities that you would like to have may be different. One of your first projects will be to explore the current limits of what you can do and speak to your spirit team about your hopes in development.

At the moment you may only have the vaguest hints as to where your future work with spirit lies, so it is important to find out where to start and who with. A good starting point is to attend your local spiritualist church. I know many people these days are put off by the word church but you will find that the spiritualist churches are different to many more orthodox churches. You will not have to adhere to doctrines or creeds, and you need only accept what you feel is true. This is important as you will not, and should not, be pushed into something you do not believe.

Each time you attend you will generally see a different medium and be able to consider which methods are the ones which come most naturally to you. Each medium will work in a different way. Their personalities come across in the way they demonstrate, and this is important to you as you move forward. Your future tutors should not try to mould you in their image, just advise you on the best way they feel you should practice.

My personal preference is that you start with people around you who are working with spirit already, so an awareness group or maybe an open circle in the churches is a good way to begin. If these are not available to you think about what working with spirit means. Investigate this. Reading the Silver Birch books is a gentle way to start, and of course there is no pressure put on you, or you putting on yourself, in just reading a book.

If you decide to start the process of working towards becoming a medium after seeing others work, the first stage is normally to join an awareness circle. Here your group leader will take you through various exercises often using tools, so you might find yourself reading cards, using ribbons or trying psychometry.

Most sessions start with a visualisation, similar to a meditation but more active. There may be some work in small groups of two, three or four where you make your first attempts at giving messages. Usually at this stage you will be using the psychic faculty and this means you will be giving information about your sitter. The logic behind this is that that you are learning to understand and work with a different energy to yourself. We interact with people all the time but this is on a more personal level. Once you have learnt to 'read' the information in the energy of your sitter, and this may take some time, the next stage is to learn how to work with the energy of someone in spirit.

You may spend some time in awareness before linking with spirit, don't worry, this is normal and you need to move forward at your own rate.

The awareness group is where mediumship begins as you will be acting as the medium between the spirit energy and your sitter. The great change is that you will start giving information about a loved one in spirit not about your sitter. At this time your tutor should advise you to move on to the next stage.

Let's get on to some basic tips for when you start out.

Be in the right place

Search out a group, church or circle that suits you. This is not as easy as you might think and you might have to try out quite a few. The aims of each group may not be right for you.

Some groups may have a gentle approach where you are comfortable at once which is a good start but many such groups have no ambition and have no history of producing capable mediums. By their fruits shall you know them. This type of group could well be good for you if you just want to sit with spirit and you could benefit a lot by getting used to spirit for a year or two. However as soon as you decide to move forward you will need to find another group which is more focused on moving the members forward.

There is no reason you have to stop going to the first one so your next group might well be 'as well as' rather than 'instead of'. When you do move on to your next stage it's a good idea to investigate who is teaching or leading the group. Good questions to ask are. Does the tutor have experience of working publicly? Do they still do this? How big is the group? This will give you an idea of how much personal attention and help you will get. Do people stay in the group? All these questions are relevant so don't be shy in asking.

The early groups are generally given the title Awareness Groups. They are an ideal place to start and you will practice feeling the energy and often work with tools. As you progress from your awareness group to a development group you will need these less and less as your trust in spirit grows.

As well as finding the right physical place also ensure that your mind is in the right place. Are you ready? Is your life able to support an extra activity? Most importantly how do you feel about it?

Find yourself a spirit buddy

When you decide to take the plunge and decide to visit your first medium or go to a spiritualist service or demonstration find a friend to go along with you. Lots of people find it difficult to go to somewhere new alone, especially when it might be full of very strange people (By the way, we are not all strange, often very different, but not all strange.) If you are especially sensitive to going somewhere new, this can be an indication that you have potential as part of developing is becoming more sensitive in many ways.

We all need support in new adventures and having a friend sharing the start of our journey is a comfort. Hopefully they will be starting their own journey too but after you have started it is easier to find pals along the way and progress is always good when you can share your successes with a friend, and of course with a good friend you can share your failures too without criticism; and you will feel that you have failed from time to time, we all do.

You and your buddy can take opportunities to see lots of mediums work. All will be different and this will give you an idea of how you would like to work yourself. With a buddy you get the chance to talk about each medium and you will find that you might like some things about one medium and they will think someone else does it better. This is where you get your first insight into both the delivery and accuracy of various mediums. You will also see that some see a lot, others hear and still more are clairsentient[9] in that they feel either emotions, physical conditions or both. If you do attend church services you will also see that some mediums give a talk from their own thoughts and some are actually inspired by spirit. Inspiration is a lovely form of mediumship to encourage in yourself.

So, if you can, find a spirit buddy, maybe you can grow together.

Prioritise

It's very easy for working with spirit to become all-consuming and can be really addictive, so we have to be considerate of all aspects of our lives. It is best to ensure your family is the top priority in your life. Your income is important too, you have to live. So, at best your work with spirit is in third place.

We did not come down to earth to become mediums, we came to experience all aspects of life from despair to rapture. Live your life first then if you can, spare a little time to be an agent of the divine. That is what mediums are!

Set your intent

When you decide to find out whether you can be a medium that is the time you need to set your intent. At this point you might not even know if you can or not but don't let this stop you wishing to be as good as you can be. So set your intention which would fulfil your wildest dreams; why not? Give yourself plenty of time to pursue your intention, we never stop learning. Also don't be shy

---

[9] A person who senses emotional and physical conditions from the spirit.

about having really high aspirations, nobody else need ever know anyway. I have had several people come to me very early on in their progression and say 'I want to be the best healer ever', is that arrogant? No, I don't believe so, it is an honest aim, an honourable intention, and if we get a little bit carried away when we see the miracles of working with spirit, who can blame us? We need to progress both as a species and as individuals and we won't advance as a species unless people work to fulfil their dreams. Do we mock athletes who have shown similar dedication and won Olympic medals? No, we don't, so there is no reason to dishonour those with a similar drive to be the best in our field.

So, set your intent and do your best, nobody can ask more.

Where are you going?

Think also, where do you want to go? At the same sort of time that you are setting your intent you should also consider where you wish to go with it and does your natural ability align with your hopes. Sometimes they may be different but in time they will naturally blend together. I believe that this is because your sprit team know your intentions and abilities and work to bring out the best in both so you reach the best outcome.

The early focus of most groups is spirit communication and newcomers tend to follow this lead. Most think, 'can I really contact the spirit world?' Well, yes, there are many ways of contacting and working with spirit. As well as using messages to heal grief and dispel fear of dying, spirit doctors and ministering angels are always on hand to help those in mental or physical distress. As a healing medium, should you want to follow that path, you are able to work with these formidable powers. Some people are able to paint or draw those in spirit. Others follow criminal investigations, yet more write and speak under inspiration.

Have a basic plan and put it into action, but allow yourself to be open to other possibilities which may develop, or you find you have already available to you.

Find your niche

As you are working to find out where you are going, you will probably find that your strengths become apparent quite quickly. I always advise you to find your niche within what is opening out for you. As you are an individual there has never been anyone quite like you and to a certain extent you will have aspects of, or a blend of your abilities which are unique, so find out where you are best suited and concentrate on this. As you grow to become proficient in your preferred way of working you will find that extra skills naturally occur as well. Focus first on your strongest areas and move on to other things later.

Read lots of books about spirit

There are huge numbers of books available about the lives of mediums and spiritual phenomena, reading some of them will help you not to put a limit on what can be achieved.

The early history of Modern Spiritualism is full of many types of mediumship rarely used today. Some things go out of fashion and some are more difficult to achieve today with our modern lives and particularly interference from electrical items. Anyway, in the past physical mediumship was more prevalent and it is very interesting to read about this. There were many notable scientists investigating the contact between the two worlds at the time.

Nowadays the accent is on evidential mental mediumship and there are many mediums currently working who give astounding evidence. The road to mediumship is rarely easy and many of the earlier mediums had to get past the views of established religions even more so than today. I find that reading about the lives of mediums from the past is especially helpful and inspiring, and helpful for the progress of us all.

Reading of the lives of the mediums of the past brings a lot of what we do into focus. I would advise looking up Eileen Garratt, Edgar Cayce, Gladys Osbourne Leonard, Alec Harris, and Harry Edwards. There are so many more that it seems a shame to pick out just a few. There are also lots of books quoting the thoughts and philosophy of Spirit Guides. Most notably I find for beginners is the range of books featuring the teachings of Silver Birch.

Practice sitting in the stillness

For some people this means meditation and others use active visualisation which I talk about later but when you start just sitting in the quiet neither searching for inner peace nor reaching out to spirit is a good way to start. A great part of learning to bring spirit to you is learning to be comfortable with your mind at peace. If you can sit with a still mind every day even for just a few minutes it will help you to be in a good place to start working. So, take what time you can to sit in the quiet. This can lead to other things and the next stage is sitting with spirit.

Be aware of obsession

Working with spirit and having a link with the Divine is a powerful thing and brings much joy and comfort. It can therefore act like a drug and become an obsession. I mentioned earlier that your family and job must have priority. You must live your life, and go through the whole gamut of emotions and experience that life gives you. Even this is helpful to your development as others who have passed to spirit shared the same emotions and your memory can be used to express their feelings. It is very hard to explain anything you have not experienced so enjoy all the ups and downs of life if you can. You will be able to use all of your experiences later on.

When we begin to realise the enormity of what we do and what it brings to us and others it is so easy to become obsessed with the wonderful oneness and communion of what we do. We need to remain down to earth. This is one reason why it is good just to sit at certain times each week. Those in spirit do not need to be linking with us all the time but are grateful for any we can give. We too should be grateful that when we do open up to them, they are always there.

You will be tempted to work with spirit all day every day, don't allow this to happen. There is an exception to this later in the book when there are some tips about healing.

Keep some free time

This applies from the first time you sit in a group right through to becoming a professional medium.

We all feel better after a holiday. It is important in order to maintain a balance in our lives that we have some free time. If we can spend this in nature so much the better. It's your life, enjoy it.

See the good things around you and go back to your mediumship refreshed, uplifted with a positive attitude. So, grant yourself a holiday from time to time, you deserve it.

Accept that mediumship is natural not supernatural

Finally, for this early section of the book we need to understand that for those of us who are fortunate enough to be able to use the gift of mediumship it is absolutely natural. The fact that children have a clear mind and are more often able to perceive spirit is testament to this. Many children in fact develop a friendship with other spirit children and I have known this friendship last a lifetime.

It is the pressure of our earth lives which makes it difficult for many of us to enjoy a better link with spirit. We shouldn't think of mediumship as being exceptional, rather that it is being natural and that it is the circumstances of difficult life periods or an ill-informed cultural upbringing which stifles progress.

Be thankful that you have become enlightened enough to pursue this natural aspect of life.

Section 2: Development

Development does not imply complexity, rather a greater understanding of simplicity. (Jeremiah, authors guide)

Not all who wander are lost

Now is the time for you to move to a stage of working with the spirit world almost exclusively. You have developed an awareness of the energies around people and are able, with or without tools, to give an accurate psychic reading with perhaps mediumship involved here and there too. Just as you can blend[10] with the energy of people, so too, you can blend with the energy of those in spirit.

---

[10] A moving of the mind of the medium to the world of spirit to enable communication.

Some of the things to carry forward into development are the following.

Firstly, your intention. You will probably find that after going through awareness that your perspective has changed a little, or maybe a lot and you might place more emphasis on a different type of mediumship or where and how you want to go ahead. Now is the time to re-focus and affirm your intent.

Continue your investigations by reading. You will probably have gravitated towards certain things by now and I recommend pursuing your interest in them.

Continue sitting in the stillness.

'Keep it simple' is a good maxim. The more complicated we make it the more difficult it is to do. Your tutor will have a range of exercises. Each of your tutors will have a different style and focus but I have found that if we are to pursue mediumship it helps if we work blind, and exercises either with eyes blindfolded or with our sitter either behind us or in the next room are very helpful. These help us to focus on our spirit link[11] rather than our sitter, and therefore we receive uncluttered information. It sounds difficult but it's actually easier as we are not tempted to work in the psychic.

There is so much to development and it will take up most of this book. We are going to concentrate on what we call mental mediumship within it and mostly this will be active. Active mediumship used in communication, as opposed to passive which is used more within healing, trance and various other forms of mediumship. Here we are concentrating on the medium as being

---

[11] The person who has joined the medium from the spirit in order to give a message to a loved one on earth.

the link between those in spirit and those on earth, so working with communication. There are a host of tips following, so let's start.

Check it out

Give some thought to and examine everything you are told. (Including all the contents of this book). If something doesn't sit well with you don't throw it away but put it to one side. I had a very solid opinion on reincarnation for example, this has totally changed in the last few years as more information has come along.

You will hear and read many opinions and examples from your tutors and in books. Most of these will make sense straight away but some will be currently beyond your understanding. That's fine. Just put such things to one side. They will probably crop up later and be more in line with your increased knowledge. Your best source of knowledge is your own experience. This will be unique. There is too much information out there for one human mind to have all knowledge and understanding. Build upon your own experience by talking to others you can trust. And, of course, you can always trust your spirit team.

Keep it simple

It is very important that as you move from working in the psychic to developing mediumship that you keep it simple. It is not necessarily easy but the basics are always the same. You, as the medium in the centre with spirit on one side and your sitter on the other. You are the link between the two, nothing more. Always bear in mind though that this doesn't mean we have to be too humble, we are just as important as the other links in the chain.

Trust your spirit team to deal with the details as there is so much potential information to be passed on. The paradox is that although simplicity is the key to your developing skills, you could end up giving every detail of the lives of your links in spirit, the features, activities and character from birth to old age. Each link can be hugely complex, trust your spirit team to sort this out and pass on the best information to help your sitter identify who wants to talk to them. So; simple in process but hugely complex in the amount of detail.

La-la land

Following on from the simplicity is the fact that you will meet many people who want to complicate things by bringing in myths. One of your roles will be to dispel such things and be an agent not just for spirit but also for truth. We work with the universal consciousness, infinite in its power, surely that is enough for anyone.

There are lots of people around will talk about faeries, unicorns and dragons, they will try to lure you in to their false concepts usually for money. Just don't go there. There never has been, nor ever will be, such a thing as a dragon.

Imagine the despair in your guides when they have worked with you to improve and when you suddenly feel this surge in power and you attribute it to a dragon. For goodness sake. This is a slap in the face to those who work with you. Stay on planet earth, la la land may be a nice place to visit but don't live there. Pursue the truth.

Assess and confirm your commitment to spirit

Once you have decided to try to develop as a medium you need to set a certain commitment in terms of the time you can spend sitting[12] and when and where that should be. It is better to start small and extend if you are able to later. If you try to do too much you will become stressed, and if you feel you should be somewhere else, for example with your family, then you are unlikely to do yourself justice when practising.

Once you establish a time and place keep that commitment. If it is just an hour a week so be it, that's fine. Don't forget that those who work with you in spirit have lived on earth too and understand your needs.

Decide what type of medium you want to be

We looked at this in the first section and in a sense, this is an ongoing thing to consider. As you move into development you will perhaps already have found some unexpected abilities or affinities to certain areas. It's good to read up on mediums in the past who have worked in a similar way, and also see if you can witness others who are currently working the way you would like to.

In the words of The Rolling Stones, 'you can't always get what you want, but if you try sometimes you might find you get what you need.' Your spirit friends will always try to help with what you want but also bring in what you need or bring in an area where you can excel.

Although this book is geared mainly to developing towards working publicly with demonstrations or private readings there are many other ways to work both publicly and in private. For example, some mediums work on crime solving and I know throughout the world that police forces use mediums on occasion. Sometimes, but

---

[12] A meeting with an individual who hopes for a link with someone in spirit. The act of being in a group, usually sitting in a circle.

not always, to very good effect. How about trying spirit art, or remote viewing?

Once you have developed your connection with spirit you will feel the right way to go for you. If you are inclined to a more passive form of mediumship, maybe you would like to try healing, inspired writing or speech. Your tutor should be able to help you decide.

Establish your preparation technique

Before you start any work with spirit prepare your mind and have a short period of calm. This will vary from individual to individual and also for the type of work you are doing, over time this period will become shorter as you attune with spirit better.

If you are working with healing or other forms of passive mediumship this time will be longer than with clairvoyance etc. With clairvoyance, a short period is better as you mind needs to be clear but active. As you move forward the time you need will be much shorter and even for healing it will be seconds rather than minutes. For practised public mediums the time is during the act of standing up or stepping on to the platform. This is because all the time you are sitting for development you are increasing the level of trust between you and your guides. So, use this short period of time to relax your mind and invite your helpers to come close.

You should also ask for a sign they can give you to tell you they are there and ready to work with you.

Try to be more observant in your everyday life

Could you describe your own sitting room? Try now and keep expanding until you get every feature colour of furniture and fitting, decorations, old or new items worn out things. Are things neat and tidy or more relaxed? Your contacts in spirit can give you this information. If you notice these things in everyday life it will be easier for you to be aware of them when given from a spirit contact. Everything you see, all the people you meet in life, their characters and appearance can be used by spirit to help improve your evidence. So, for example, if you were to see your own grandfather while in a sitting you can describe him and his relationship and character and be confident that this with be accurate too for the grandfather of your sitter. In time you will know when the similarities stop and different evidence unique to your contact in spirit will become apparent. So be observant of everything, it will help you immensely.

One way to build a contact

You have now reached the stage where you are working with spirit links so you need to work out your way to build up your contact. Remember that your spirit team are working to help you with this, and trust in them is paramount to success.

A good way to start is just to say, 'I have a lady with me', or you could say a child or a gentleman. Spirit will have someone ready. Then go on to say how you feel with this person, maybe their physical condition, or how you feel the relationship is. Try to give a couple more pieces of information and then put it out to your circle or audience.

You can of course choose someone to go to directly, but at this stage I find it is very easy to slip into working psychically when you do this, and at this time you are moving to working with spirit a greater proportion of the time. Concentrate on your link with spirit and they will locate your recipient by feeding you relevant information.

In your groups the people around you should be told to be as positive as they can. If you were to start by saying firstly that you have a lady, everyone should be able to say yes. Then maybe a condition, say they had cancer, now some you will lose, but most people know a lady who has passed with cancer. Then maybe a relationship, say an aunt, your responses will gradually lessen until you have just one or two. Then you give a further piece of information, and as your link will have strengthened by this time this may well be something significant which identifies your link in spirit. The more you practice this the better and quicker it will be.

Once you have identified your sitter the information should start to flow. Remember that your concentration must always remain with your link in spirit not your sitter.

Use surprising thoughts

We have spoken of how spirit will use all your experiences to help with links when there are similarities they can exploit. The opposite is also true, they will give you surprising things you would never think of. It is therefore obvious that it comes from spirit. Be confident in passing this information on.

This applies to when you are training and also when you are a practising medium on the rostrum. At the moment you are sitting in circle and practicing to give a link.

Imagine you are all in a quiet state going through your preparation when suddenly in your mind's eye you see a big red bus. This is not your mind wandering, it is a sign that you are in the correct state to work and that your guides can place a thought in your mind.

When the opportunity arises, as maybe someone else is speaking or you are all in preparation, give out the information and it will be relevant to someone present. A key phrase here is 'if it is not your thought where did it come from?'

Use all five senses

Try to be aware of all your senses in everyday life and transfer this into your mediumship. We often speak of hearing and seeing information but little is said about taste and smell. If for example you smell flowers during your description of someone bring it in to the conversation.

It is best in this situation not to say why am I smelling flowers, but say to your sitter, 'and as I am speaking about so and so, you would understand why I am smelling flowers.' This is far more positive.

If we use this as a further example and feel into the fragrance, we may be able to say the type of flower we are smelling and this would perhaps be the persons favourite. If there is a blend of many scents then maybe the link worked in a florist or had many varieties in their garden. When you feel into the evidence of the smell this will become more and more clear. This is why it is important to sit in circle to practice as you can develop your skills with no pressure upon you.

When you use all five senses you can build up a much fuller picture of your link and give your sitter a much better experience. Now let's look at your methods more closely.

Don't just rely on seeing

If you are lucky enough to have objective clairvoyance[13], that is you can actually see people and things in the room this is very good mediumship, but it has pitfalls so let's go into this a little.

---

[13] A person who can see energy from spirit.

Firstly, you have a wonderful gift to use, not many people have this facility. However, a picture is just that, like a photo it can be very accurate but has no soul or character. There are several ways to develop this great start.

Use the picture itself to give information. Try to go into detail, and as you do more and more will become apparent. At some point though you will have to move from the picture into areas giving a full appreciation of what this person was like. The picture will represent a certain time and often this will be a shared memory with your sitter. You will learn to feel into the picture. For example, if you see them in a hospital bed try to feel who was present, what was said, what the physical problem was. When you feel into the picture you can also feel into the character, home, hobbies and work of the person.

Explore their character with your feelings as their whole life is in that picture when you seek it out. When you do this, you have moved from the original viewing into the energy of spirit.

The problem is that if you see so clearly you will tend to rely just on the picture. In order to give a good reading, it is important to find out the meaning to it.

Go to the movies

Most clairvoyance is seen in the mind's eye. This is called subjective clairvoyance. Just as the mediums who can see objectively, that is outside, give what details you can about your vision. Don't miss out on the information that is there.

Let's use a picture of a car as an example. You see a car.

Ask questions. What colour? What make and model? How many doors? What is the licence plate number? Look at the dashboard.

How many miles are on the clock? Describe the dashboard. Then move into clairsentience.

How does the car make you feel? Was it much loved? Was in perhaps involved in a collision, so look for any faults. Did the owner maintain it themselves or was it always taken to a mechanic? If the owner maintained it, did they help neighbours out too? Use everything you can as there will be a gem of information there, otherwise why would your link show it to you?

Once you see a picture you can also ask your spirit team to expand on this and maybe present a video. This will normally be a significant time in the life of your link, something like a wedding or a first meeting. Yes, this can be achieved but be patient. Once you start receiving a picture speak to your guide about developing it in this way. They will do their best to help.

A very common mistake with pictures is to think they are symbolic. Remember we are practising evidential mediumship. Everything you receive should be relevant to your link in spirit.

It's more than a feeling

Once you have moved into the power, either publicly or in a circle or a one-to-one situation, everything you see hear and most importantly feel is relevant. Clairsentience is the most common and most underrated form of mediumship yet this is where the link you have in spirit becomes a real person, with physical feelings and emotions. This is the area too where as a medium you become most aware of your link and ultimately can blend with the person, not just look from outside or hear but become immersed in their energy.

When you achieve this, you have the whole of their lives available. You will find that you are prompted to give certain pieces of information. It is impossible for you to give details of a whole life in ten minutes or even in a half hour sitting.

The link will give you what they think is most relevant or most important to them. The downfall is that what was a very important moment for them might not have been for your sitter and could have been almost instantly forgotten. So, either you need to find the context or just ask your sitter to put it to one side for a while.

I have mentioned that everything is relevant and all the information you receive will be; the forgotten item may well be placed later on in the reading. With clairsentience you will often feel the physical conditions of your link and this can give you actual pain. It helps that once you have recognised each condition the effect will continue to lessen both for that condition and in general. In the end it is just a knowing that the person suffered this or that ailment.

In using your clairsentient ability, you can turn an unremarkable reading into something truly special. It is the difference between your client returning home and saying, 'Oh by the way dad came through' and 'Oh my God, dad was there, it was amazing!'

This is why we do the work, to touch the souls of others. If we do our job well your sitters understanding of the spirit world will grow.

Share any emotion you feel

When you stand up to give a message, even in a group, you will feel an emotion. Sometimes this is your own but often it is an emotion that your link felt, how do you differentiate between the

24

two? It can be surprisingly easy. For example, if you are usually nervous when you stand up and this time you are not, why is that? The person you have with you was a confident individual, this is your first piece of information. Of course, on many occasions you will feel a love towards your sitter, in fact this is so common that it is not very evidential. It is natural that your family (and others) love you so always give this out anyway but only if you feel it.

There are other emotions that can identify who you have with you. Anxiety, worry, a compassion for people and animals, those who carry a vibrant encouraging emotion often come through when your sitter is in need of upliftment.

From these emotions you can investigate why they were the way they were and this will bring more information about their lives. It may be that the person felt hopeless. This could be due to financial problems, if so, what was the cause, redundancy, loss of a partner, it could be that the person had too much responsibility at home or work. When you feel into the causes of the emotion you can find good evidence.

This also often shows an understanding by the person in spirit of the issues that your sitter is currently having to deal with. Another common emotion we come across is guilt, either by the spirit who mistreated your sitter in some way and is seeking forgiveness or that your sitter is feeling guilty that they did not do enough for your spirit link when they were in need.

There is always forgiveness from spirit in these circumstances.

Be conscious of gestures

Gestures creep up on you without you knowing. There you are, happily going along in you reading and you start wringing your hands, scratching your head, and once for me very embarrassingly picking your nose! I believe that as we are not conscious of the gestures, but spirit are able to produce them as long as we are free of thought about them.

Be aware of what you are doing, as gestures can be very singular and it gives your sitter a great deal of evidence when they can actually see you copy what their loved one did.

Use all the clairs (except one)

As well as the usual senses of seeing feeling and hearing, the rest of our senses can be used. Most often taste and smell, called clairgustance[14] and clairolfactence[15].

Receiving tastes or smells during giving a reading is not especially common and is often overlooked, but for some people these can be significant pieces of evidence. The fragrance of a certain perfume can be the specific piece of evidence which identifies one person from another when there is doubt.

The taste of a certain food can be the same. Many people have one or two favourite meals or food items. A good practice for clairolfactence is to sit in the power with your guide and see if you can smell them. This has to be done not by trying but by allowing their presence to manifest.

Much of all mediumship is learning to allow things to happen rather that reaching out too strongly.

What is the one clair you should not use? It is the most common, called clairdelusion. This is when your active mind takes over from

---

[14] The ability to pick up taste from spirit.
[15] The ability to pick up scents and smells from spirit.

your contemplative state of awareness of spirit. It then takes you on a journey of thought following your own experiences.

It is very difficult when you are learning to dispel these thoughts, it can only come by practice. You will learn to feel when the emphasis has changed and your tutor will help. When you have received a series of yes's and suddenly you have a series of noes then you will realise that you have gone off track.

Restart your procedure of linking with spirit and move your mind to them, this will re-establish your link.

Try not to think

This is not easy, try it now!

Not easy is it?

The medium thinking can be the cause of a poor sitting. As in the previous point it is in allowing not thinking that we achieve our best results.

A good practice is to meditate just on clearing your mind and letting any thoughts slip by. Focus on your breathing, your thoughts will gradually melt away.

Once you are able to do this it will help your presentation and stop your inquisitive mind gaining control. This allows the spirit influence to become stronger and therefore your messages become both more accurate and more detailed. Remember that it is the quality of our evidence which brings proof of survival.

Apart from the actual mechanics of mediumship there are lots of things to develop and observe. This is part of the personal development which helps you along the way. The path of the medium is much more than the mechanics. The fact that we are working with divine agents rubs off. Our personal development as people with compassion and understanding helps us become better human beings.

Try to be patient

Mediumship brings a whole lifetime of opportunity. Your mediumship will flourish at the right time. We often speak of being patient with distaste but it is important to allow your unfoldment go at its own pace. All the people around you will grow at a different rate dependant on the natural level of blending, the amount of time each is able to commit and their outside life. It can take many years of hard work before your own flower blossoms but this time is never wasted.

A strong foundation will bring a strength in your mediumship which those who rush on will never enjoy.

It's not a race

Following on from your personal patient approach you will find a steady improvement. There will always be people around you who seem to develop more quickly, or indeed less quickly than yourself. Be happy for one and supportive of the other.

Don't be dragged into a race by your natural competitiveness. The competition is actually with yourself, and the prize is to be the best you can be, not how others are. Embrace your unique set of attributes. Quality is always better than quantity. If you want to progress more quickly try to find more time to sit with spirit.

Look to your strengths

The easiest way to develop is to concentrate on improving your natural strengths. Many often try to improve areas of weakness as a way to generally improve but if you have areas you are good at it will be more natural and therefore easier to practice these in order to improve. This is true in most aspects of life so it should come naturally to you.

Use this method especially early in your development when you need to help your self-esteem. If for example you are able to feel the physical conditions of your link, then concentrate on that. Examine the feelings, identify the causes. You will find that by focusing on your strengths you will be able to be accurate enough to identify your link. Job done. This will give you the confidence to then expand into other areas where you are not so sure. Trust this process and your spirit team. Once you gain confidence moving into associated areas will be easier.

Learn speaking and presentation skills

Ask your tutor to include presentation skills within your development. This is helpful when you first start working with the public. Most of us dread standing up in front of an audience or congregation and this fear does not help our work. Basic skills such as speaking to the back of the room and engaging everyone in the room with eye contact help you overcome any problems.

Part of taking a church service, if ever you do, involves giving a fifteen minute philosophical address. This sounds dreadful at first but a good tutor will help you with this. Gestures are good but habits are not. No matter how nervous you feel, speak with confidence, and pretend the people at the back are deaf. Even if you feel dreadful don't be a wilting wallflower and mumble. Gain strength from your spirit team and from your own preparation.

In time you will be able to just speak off the cuff inspired by your guides. Until then your watchword should be prepare. You can practice in front of a mirror too. So the two important words for you are prepare and practice. It is important not to skimp this. Make sure that as you step up to speak you are ready and as confident as you can be.

The address in a service comes before your demonstration. If you give a good confident address your audience will be confident in you when your time comes to give messages. It helps a lot to have the audience on your side.

Give recognition

Give thanks to your friends and helpers in spirit, everyone needs recognition, even those who have gone before, so remember to thank your team after your demonstration. Try also to give recognition to yourself for a job well done. No-one else knows what efforts you have made to get where you are.

Often, after a service or a demonstration your chairperson will give thanks, both publicly and privately. These are special moments for you to treasure.

Think too of how those who are learning with you are feeling. They are sharing your emotions so it's good to compliment them when they do well.

A point here is that as you work with spirit you will become more sensitive. Your recognition and confidence needs to grow alongside this extra sensitivity. As you receive more and more thanks you will become more and more confident and this can only help your mediumship.

Don't keep your worries to yourself

Share any negative thoughts or worries with others. You will generally be doing better than you give yourself credit for. Your circle leader should help, and remember your spirit buddy from the earlier section? Chat with them about any worries about your progress, and share your successes too.

We all receive some hard knocks in the course of progress and question our ability and worthiness. These questions are natural. You don't have to measure your progress against others. We are all at different stages of progress and unfoldment of our latent abilities. Admire and encourage the others.

A good chat after your meetings is a great way to assuage your worries. You might find that while you are worrying that you are not keeping up, there will be others who wish they could do what you can. Share your worries. You will be surprised sometimes by what answers you receive from your compatriots. It is so easy to see what others can do, and strangely difficult to monitor our own progress.

Trust the unusual

The more unusual the information you receive is the greater its value as evidence. This is why it is so important to develop trust in the rapport between you and your spirit team. You will need to build up your confidence in order to give off something very strange. Unusual memories, symptoms or events really help a member of your audience to identify themselves with your link.

A very early example of this occurred in my own development when I first worked publicly. I was sharing the platform with my mentor and asked if I had a link. All I saw was three elephants walking along a road. Naturally I was hesitant to jump up and say that, but plucking up courage I did. It turned out to be extremely relevant and I then saw a clown and the people who were there with the sitter, who were the messengers from spirit. By the nature of the vehicles in the street I managed to identify the era too.

The lesson here was to trust my team. It takes a long time to develop such trust in an unseen person but if you keep passing on the information you receive this trust will grow. Remember, the more unusual, the more influential the information is.

Remember spirit can use your life experiences

Most lives go through some similar experiences, some can be almost identical. If you have a close sibling the chances are that you have shared a great many exploits and routine situations too.

We are using mental mediumship and this to a greater or lesser extent involves a blending of minds. That of your spirit helper, the link in spirit and your own. Where there are shared experiences it is easier for spirit to use your memories to bring forward their own.

Imagine you had an uncle who was in the navy and you see a picture of him in your mind, your sitter will have knowledge of a similar person. Keep giving the information you have about your uncle until you feel the next piece will be wrong. It is unlikely that you would see your uncle if they only had the navy in common so you can rely on having several pieces of information available. At the point the similarities end, feel into the link to get further information specific to your sitters uncle not your own.

There are many areas of your own life that spirit can use, this may be books you have read, music you like or dislike, places you have visited. It helps if you can develop as broad a view of life as possible. The more you experience of life the better your rapport with those in spirit will be.

Don't embellish or interpret

There is a common saying in mediumship which is 'Say what you see' (Or feel or hear). This is good advice. It is understandable that we wish to give our sitters the best experience possible, and there is a temptation to make things sound better, but every time we deviate from what information we are given, we move away from the truth and this can have grievous consequences. When you receive a piece of information feel into it to see what else there is. If you feel nothing more leave it. It will probably be strong enough to stand alone.

Many messages have been spoilt by the medium saying 'This always means this to me', in this case it might not, it may be that the information you gave had a special significance to your sitter, and if you interpret it your way a great piece of evidence is lost.

Feeling into your evidence rather than letting your mind wander is very hard to achieve but a good way to deal with this is practice in your group. You will need a strong partner who is prepared to give you a strong 'No' when the information is wrong.

Allow your mind to wander after each piece of information. There will be a different feeling in the information before a 'No' than a 'Yes'. It takes a lot of practice to feel the difference for some. Others adapt quickly but everyone will need to spend some time refining this.

Don't be surprised

At some point you will receive information either of a type you have not experienced before or receive it in a new way. Sometimes people can be reluctant to give off this new information, mainly due to lack of confidence. Again, trust comes in here, give off the information. You may find that in circle someone else gives the same information that you had and did not say, then you think to yourself 'I had that', and then you beat yourself up for not giving it. Try not to do that, just take it as confirmation that you did indeed have the information and be more confident in voicing it next time.

These new ways of working can occur at any time. Let's take for example the scenario of being in a circle. You might be quite happy with giving your normal range of information but you have never given a name or relationship. (Many fine mediums have never given a name). All of a sudden you hear 'Uncle Jack', don't be surprised, you have been hoping for names and relationships for a year or two.

Don't be surprised, this is what you have worked for, accept it and move on to the next surprise.

This type of event can happen in any area of your work in your sensing, hearing and vision. The more you sit the more frequent these events become, so, don't be surprised, be happy. Your commitment has paid off.

Practice, practice, practice

The great South African golfer Gary Player famously said, 'the more I practice the luckier I get'.

This applies to many things and is no different when working with spirit. The more time you can spend working in your groups or sitting alone the better your rapport with spirit will be. I am including spending time to read about spiritual things and people in your time of contemplation and expansion.

If you are able to attend courses or workshops then make the most of that too.

Don't despair

We have all been there, in the depths of despair, everyone else seems better, we can't locate our recipient, 'I'm just not good enough'.

Most of the time we don't realise the progress we are making and long periods are spent in preparation. This is one of the reasons for you to find a spirit buddy, they will be going through the same things too and will see more of your progress than you do yourself. It's easier to see progress from outside.

Your time sitting is never wasted and the longer the preparation the greater the ability when it comes. Consider the physical mediums who sit for many years with nothing to show, but when it arrives it is spectacular.

Don't despair, you are never alone.

Regularly reassess your goals

This does not necessarily mean change them. You might well have become more proficient in a certain area which does not quite follow your plan. You may need to change your focus slightly to realign your progress to your intention.

Another reason is that you may have set the bar too low and already have achieved what you set out to do. In this case, yes, do look again and set a different intention that perhaps will take longer to achieve. Remember your potential has no limits. You have achieved your first ambition. Take a clear look at what you have done and what you would like to do next. You might want a change of direction.

I once sat in circle with a lady who received lots of information at home but very little in circle. Then, one evening we decided to sit for a more passive form of mediumship including healing. Her power was truly amazing, she had found her true gift unlooked for.

Just as in the earlier tip, expect the unexpected!

Make the most of your meetings

In groups it is not just about your own progress but the group as a whole will become more and more proficient.

Your group will have several individuals who will all work in different ways, even within a single exercise. They will all get information in different ways. Look which way is most efficient or most evidential. If you see someone working in a way you like, put the thought out to your guides to add this method to your own abilities. This applies both to the type of information you receive and the way you receive it. This will strengthen the link in your team and will help your mediumship to be expressed in a more complete way.

Don't be discouraged

There will be times when you feel that you have not progressed for a while, that your mediumship has stagnated. Keep your faith and don't be discouraged, there are better times ahead.

Development is about preparation, it's not easy. Look back on where you were when you started. When you are flat for a while there is normally a significant change for the better at the end of it. Talk to your buddies and members of your group about it but most of all sit with your guides. Talk to them even if you can't hear their reply, and look forward to that next leap forward.

Use the dynamics of your group to move forward

Be inspired by the success of others.

As you start out on your journey of development you will find yourself in a group of people. This may be small in number or quite large. The one sure thing is that it will be in a constant state of evolution. Members will change, the group may merge, split, and rejoin, grow, and shrink constantly as each person finds their way forward. Situations change in most people's lives quite often and some may leave for a period of years before their life allows them to restart. This is fine. When the time is right they will blossom.

It is important that you bring a positive energy into the groups you are involved in. Be keen to learn. There are lots of techniques out there and just as each medium is unique so too is each teacher. Everyone will work a little differently.

Some groups sit for years without producing a medium. Their emphasis is sitting in the comfort of spirit, in a calm social environment. This too has its purpose but if you are hoping to move forward this type of group is not for you and you need to work in more dynamic surroundings.

There will come a time when you need to expand, just like moving from primary to secondary education then on to college and university. Each stage is helpful to you but comes to a natural end.

Use the experience of those you know who have taken these steps before you. They will advise on where your abilities can best be developed. At each stage try to be a positive influence to those around you, encourage others and take a pride in the group's performance, even though you may be just a small part of it. Your time will come.

Don't be afraid to move up when the time is right, a good tutor will know when that is, as they will when you are ready to serve the churches or meeting places. They will advise you when you are ready to move on.

Most of the time in your journey invitations will arrive as you progress. Feel into these invitations as you would into a link with spirit some will be good for you, some will not. Be guided to the right place. If you find you are in a group who are there to serve their own self esteem rather than spirit, (and there are such people), don't hesitate - move on.

Encourage others

If there is anything worse than not receiving recognition for your efforts it is not having support when your efforts don't go as you would like. Your group leader should know when someone is feeling down and offer help but it is good to receive help from your peers, so make an effort to console anyone who is going through a difficult stage. It happens to us all from time to time.

Everyone in every session has done something well, even if it is making the tea afterwards! Let them know. Let them know also if you have noticed that they have taken a step forward on their path. In short, be nice.

Make a point of seeing other mediums in several venues

Each medium and each venue is different, venues can be large or cosy and each has its own feel. It's good practice to pick up the energies of different places. In the future you will hopefully be working in many places and you will be comfortable to work in all of them.

Mediums all have their own idiosyncrasies, but most of the methods are the similar. Each will have built up their own library but there will always be extra new pieces of information for them to store.

Methods differ, many mediums go direct to a person, either directed by spirit or through choice. This can be very helpful much of the time. The danger with it is that it is very tempting to drop into working psychically when you do this. You may be looking directly at someone, feel a pull in that direction and the details you give are meaningless to the person you choose, but apply properly to someone sitting directly behind your false recipient. This is unsettling and can affect your confidence. If you can go direct and are regularly successful carry on.

The second method is that you establish your initial link with spirit and pass on the information you receive to everyone in the room. You may receive several responders to start with, but with each piece of information their numbers will reduce. Feel for a specific piece of information that will identify your link with one person. Later on, you might be able to give a message to everyone who raises their hand.

When you witness someone working in a way that especially pleases you, put a thought out to your guide that you would like to work that way too. It won't be quite the same because you are you, but your team will work with you to build up the method to allow you to take up that way of working.

As a rule, I advocate establishing a link with spirit before reaching out to the audience. Others may disagree and that's ok.

Build your library

When you start giving messages from spirit you will find that some items crop up more than once. Your spirit team are learning what you can receive. Remember your circles are training grounds for your development. If you have for example been able to describe a scene quite clearly don't be surprised if you see that same scene again quite soon. This is what we call building up your library.

This will happen maybe many times as you develop different methods to give information. You may feel a heart condition and correctly say it was a heart attack. The next week you may get another and then yet another. As this progresses you will feel whether this was fatal or not. Whether the heart condition was known about et cetera. The feeling of the heart attack will be the entry you put into your library the rest of the interpretation is about the particular link you are working with.

There is no limit to what can be in your library, it can end up being vast, comprising taste and scents as well as feelings words and visions.

There is one danger to be aware of in that it is easy to take the comparison too far. Don't presume each time an item from your library crops up it will be identical to before. If you do not feel into the specific circumstances of the event you can miss out on particular information.

A second thing to be aware of is that it is possible to rely on what you know and ignore new things you are receiving, in other words don't let your library become your comfort zone. Always be prepared for development. That is why you practice.

Try to use numbers

Numbers can be a very quick and accurate way to identify your contact. Dates, especially birthdays, are often remembered by family members who may be present.

The same applies to house numbers, car registration plates and numerous other items. If you happen to see a gathering around someone's deathbed in hospital, count the people around the bed, but don't just focus on that. Look at the walls and see a calendar and a clock. This will give you the time and date of their passing.

Telephone numbers too can be fabulous evidence. I once witnessed a well-known medium give a young lady the telephone number of her recently deceased boyfriend. The number was still stored in her phone and corresponded exactly.

This is a good point to remember. If spirit can give you three digits, they can give you twelve, don't limit spirit. Furthermore, it follows that if they can give you a month, they can give you the day, and the time.

Don't be satisfied giving a month, almost everyone can find a birthday in every month with little effort. It is therefore not evidential at all. Throwing out months is not the level of competence we seek. It's waffle. Do we want to be waffly mediums**? No, we don't!**

Explore colour when you see it

With many potential mediums colour is the first thing they see, as perhaps at the early stages of awareness the energy of the various colours becomes apparent to them. I believe that when you work with colour the most important thing is feeling into the meaning. This will be slightly different every time as the unique blend of the spirit in contact with you, and your recipient will be represented in it.

Therefore, it is important not to say that a colour always means a certain thing. There are countless shades of every colour, and all will feel a little different. If we as the mediums are not adaptable to this, we can easily miss the special significance the colour may have for the recipient about their loved ones. Feel for the special significance.

There are many ways that colour can really help identifying your link and their character. You may be aware of several pastel shades which your link might have enjoyed. If so, did they perhaps paint in pastel shades or did they like to wear them. Would this be also an indication of a gentle character, and likewise would lots of primary colours indicate a dominant confident person?

Treat each aspect of colour with care, and be open to a multitude of possibilities.

Colour brings so much depth to your mediumship. Imagine special memories linked to a fairground, a beautiful garden, the night sky or even more mundane things such as home decorations. Shared memories of these can be very special.

The use of colour in your mediumship can lead to so many parts of your mediumship beginning to flower and from time to time will bring forward something so significant it will be the highlight of your reading.

Grandmothers are special people

Grandmothers seem to have a special place in the hearts of many people, so it is not surprising that they come through a lot. They are also likely to be the members of your family who have passed on.

The scene is set. You are in a group and a person stands up says they are with you. Consider the two descriptions.

'I have your grandmother, she is in the kitchen baking an apple pie. She has an apron on and gives you a red rose and sends you lots of love.'

Really? Is this where we want to be. Nothing at all that identifies her as being different from any grandmother. No evidence at all about her.

All grandmothers baked the best apple pie of all time.

Now consider how it should be, this time not going direct. The medium stands up.

'I have a grandmother with me. She is standing by an oblong wooden table which is worn smooth and I can feel the grain of the wood standing proud. She is wearing an apron tied at the back and it has a pattern of two large birds on the front. She is baking an apple pie and tells me that she always used to use the spare pastry to make patterns on the top. She baked the pie on an enamel dish which had a green edge. I feel she always had the pie with cream not custard which her husband didn't like. Who am I with?'

The second medium will not get many responses. Every piece of evidence should be correct and part of a memory.

Would you rather be medium one or medium two?

You will have lots of grandmothers come through. They will each have their own story and idiosyncrasies. If after this information there is still doubt move around the home and garden. Find out her ailments. How did she get on with her husband? What was he like? Explore the whole scene.

An apron and an apple pie are just not enough information. Much more detail is required.

Remember that when in the power everything is relevant

Once you have identified the changes which signify to you that you are in contact with spirit, and therefore ready to work, everything you feel with all your senses becomes relevant to your link in spirit.

Your spirit team will bring forward your link as close as they can so you can pick up the most important things about them, to ensure that you are with the correct person and that they recognise who has come to speak to them.

Let's say that like most of us you are nervous before starting your demonstration. If when you stand up this becomes a real worry or agitation you know that your first link got agitated easily and this was a strong aspect of their character. Accept that this feeling is not yours and that spirit have emphasised your own feelings to portray your link. So then feel into the worry and agitation, what caused it, maybe too much responsibility, maybe they never had two coins to rub together. You can feel into any type of information you receive. A good point here is to think that if a feeling is not naturally yours then it comes from spirit.

Just as all feelings are important so too is a lack of feelings, physical or emotional. Some things that have happened to me are that I could not feel my feet. The link was an amputee. I also found myself unable to speak. That link was a deaf mute.

Once you can give this type of information it shows that your ability to link with spirit has grown. Make the most of these links when they occur. The more you use new things the more will become available.

It is worthwhile repeating; everything you feel when you are in the power is relevant.

Seek out the special item

To make a sitting memorable it needs to have an edge. Something out of the ordinary which could not possibly have come from the mind of you, the medium. It is not always possible to produce such an item but when you do it will bring you extra confidence.

Very often these especially significant pieces of information come in the form of joint memories. Your sitter may have several people in spirit who are similar, say a group of uncles, who had similar lives and went through the usual phases of life, school, job, marriage, divorce, remarriage etc etc. To find out which one you have with you will need a very specific piece of evidence. Even the most normal of this group of potential links will have something specific about them. There will be one thing your sitter remembers them by. You have to feel closely into the link to get them to provide that special thing. Sometimes it does not happen and you have to then find lots of smaller pieces of information, for example an address which separates the one from the others. The more unusual the special piece of information has the greater its value as evidence.

Of course, not all contacts are run of the mill. Many people in spirit were great characters with lots of unusual happenings in their lives. If only every contact were like this!

Expand on the information

This means feeling into what you are given to find facts that you weren't originally aware of. This does **not** include interpretation or embellishment from your own experience or imagination. There is always more available from what you see, hear or feel.

Let's just go into our minds eye right now. See a picture of a house for example. Is it brick, stone or wooden? Describe the frontage. How many windows are there? Are they a single pane of glass or are there several? Are there curtains or blinds behind them? Where is the door situated? Now you can see the house in your mind's eye more clearly. Approach the door. Is it painted? If so what colour. What is the door furniture like?

Knock on the door and see who lets you in or maybe it just opens. Do you enter a hallway or straight into a room? Is the floor wooden, carpeted or tiled? What furniture can you see? If you see a musical instrument, who played it? In a kitchen open the cupboards, in a bedroom open the wardrobe what do you see? You can describe the contents of a cupboard, describe the pottery and porcelain. Find out the persons favourite cup.

All these details give you more information about your link. You may find yourself drawn to a certain item of significance; you may smell a certain meal being cooked. All these things are not by chance. Your link is guiding you to areas that will establish who they are or bring back certain memories.

You may find evidence of hobbies, maybe knitting, painting crosswords, whatever you see pass it on. Is there a radio or old-fashioned record player visible? Open the cupboard part and see what records are there. Who was the person's favourite artist or type of music?

Whilst in the house, don't forget to look out the windows. Find out the location, there may be a street sign there so you can give the address. Describe the garden or yard you can do this to the same depth as the home.

All of this information will enrich your readings and this itself serves both the spirit and the sitter which is our whole purpose, to serve them both well.

This method of exploration can be applied to almost any piece of information you receive. The more you do this, the more likely you are to give that special reading, and much more frequently too.

Consider if you were the 'dead' person

Think about what information you would give through a medium if you could.

Would this information be the same for each of your friends and family? Of course not, they would have different memories of you and certainly many of your friends would have known you for a certain period of your life. So even your appearance would be different.

Some things are permanent or semi- permanent, your home could be one of these, but your character would develop through time as would any long-term ailments. So, some people would know all about you, but others perhaps only through a hobby, or shared schooldays, or time in a certain job etc. Therefore, your portrayal of yourself would be slightly different to each of the people you have met through life.

Think too now of information you would not give. Certainly, personal information about your recipient would not be mentioned in public.

Thinking about how difficult it may be to express yourself, would you talk in riddles? No of course not, so why would a medium ever say, 'oh, this is symbolic'? The answer is never, this is often a cop out. As a medium don't do it.

The only time anything should be given as symbolic is during the message at the end when to protect your recipient the symbolism will only mean something to them and no-one else. Even then, surely your link could find a more accurate way of doing things.

If you find yourself giving things as symbolic, have a thought, is this true or have I drifted off to visit la la land?

Before the message

Once you have established your contact it is a good idea to seek out a special piece of information to clear all doubt. This will give your sitter total confidence that you have the person they thought. A special item can be anything from an heirloom they have or a special memory where only the two of them were there. This one piece of information is often what brings your sitter to tears of joy because it has a special significance.

It is the 'one last thing' that you as the medium seek out and has the added benefit of giving you as the medium that little bit of extra confidence which we all need.

The gift from spirit

This will not occur in every sitting or reading but is worth seeking out. Imagine once more you are the person in spirit. As well as proving your survival of death you have given a message to your loved one. Most of us would like to give a gift too. Rather like you would send a letter and gift together in a parcel to someone.

They go well together. Feel what your link would like to give to your sitter, it might be something simple like a box of chocolates. (if so, make sure it's the right type), or could be something very special. Whatever it is it will be well received by your sitter.

Always relay the message

Sometimes, after giving lots of evidence, mediums will forget to relay the message. They have given wonderful proof of survival, but nothing personal for their sitter. There is always a message and it is never just 'hello'.

Would you take all your time proving your survival and joining the two worlds together just to say hello? Of course not. Neither will they.

You will often find that as well as feeling the urge to give a message there will be an urge to give a gift from spirit. This could be advice from a joint memory, a favourite item or even a bar of chocolate. Consider that you are the link from spirit, surely it makes sense that you would like to give a gift as well as a message. Like so many things in mediumship when subject to investigation everything makes sense.

The message is always relevant and always positive. This helps to end your reading on a positive uplifting note.

*I'm sure that you, the reader will have noticed several recurring themes within this book, and they will carry on recurring. The reason is that throughout your development from awareness to rostrum mediumship and beyond, there has to be a continuation and many things relate to various or all stages.

Practice is one of these. Maybe this seems boring, boring, boring, but although it is repetitive, each and every time you practice you are moving forward.

Another theme at many stages is that people will see your talent and will want to include you in their area or type of working. Examine these closely and get an opportunity to see them. Are they true mediums or are they trying to use your power?

Check out if they have had a one-way ticket to la la land! If what you witness with them is nonsense, quietly move away back on to your pathway with the universal consciousness. If it feels right do it, if not, don't.

Another recurring theme is the teamwork with you and your guides. Never underestimate the power of this. You are part of an amazing group and for your group, their only representative on the earth plane. Try your best to do them justice.

The main theme of all our mediumship should be truth and so I have repeatedly mentioned developing the truth around each piece of information without slipping into your own thoughts. The time to fail to do this is your time within your group. You may slip into thought many, many times before discerning the difference. This is fine so long as it is not presented as truth in public. There will come a time when you do move into something called clairknowing. You will not be aware of how you receive the information, as you will not feel see or hear it, but it is there. My own thoughts are that this is when you have developed enough to, in a sense, become that person in spirit and just relay the information. Often this provides the most astounding information. Look forward to doing this.

Sometimes nothing is everything

What do you do when you have finished one link and are moving to the next and nothing happens?

The main reason this occurs is that you have dropped out of your own link with spirit, so it is easy to quickly go through your process again until you feel spirit with you again.

There are other reasons too. Your next link may have been suffering from dementia not been aware of anything around them. If you suspect this is the case don't shy away but move closer to the link and begin to blend. You might find that they were at a state where they didn't know who they were, let alone those who were around them. I have known cases when they didn't even know what sex they were. Once you have got this information across to your sitter[16] they will start giving you still more information. So, why give you the vacant mind first? The first item is usually the most important so there will be something in the message later which refers to this.

Another case is perhaps the link was unconscious for a while before they passed to spirit. Again, this would be important to them to explain perhaps that they were aware of your sitters' presence or words that were said.

Once again, being repetitive, everything you feel when in the power is relevant even if you feel nothing. Explore this just as you would any other piece of evidence.

---

[16] The person who comes to you for a reading.

Be aware when you are inspired

At some point of your training for public mediumship your tutor will work on the inspired speech, which is a part of the spiritualist service here in the UK. Many people who are good mediums find this part of our work daunting but it really is mediumship for everyone, meant to touch all the people gathered round and about you.

Most people are reluctant to speak their thoughts in front of others but there is a way forward to this.

To start with, work without being aware of being inspired. Select an object or a subject. An object is easier at first. Describe its features and its uses. Then transfer its uses to the use we can be as human beings. For example, we can be a straight and as resilient as a brick.

Practice giving just one minute talks about mundane objects then increase this to two, five minutes etc.

The same applies to subjects you would like to talk about. Something close to your heart. Again, start with very short periods.

Next move into the power, draw your team close and repeat the exercises. Feel the differences as your team merge their thoughts to yours. Allow this blending to increase and you will begin to realise that you are using words that you wouldn't normally use and that ideas are developing beyond your normal thoughts. This is when we are working with inspiration.

Not only does this apply to speaking, but also to writing. Many mediums are inspired to write poetry or prose, and this again will start with your own thoughts and be developed as you blend with spirit more and more closely.

In my opinion much of the great poetry in the English language has been inspired in this way.

When working publicly, have a set theme with bullet points the first few times you work. You will find that new words crop up which weren't in the text as you deliver the speech. This is the start of inspiration. Allow the spirit influence to grow and you will find that somehow your words have reached and inspired many people.

It will give you a surprising amount of satisfaction the first time a member of the congregation congratulates you on your address.

As time goes by you may just have one or two words to prepare and often these will be given by spirit.

Never give up

I mentioned in the 'sometimes nothing is everything' section that we must never give up on what we are feeling and that is true.

The greater part of not giving up is not giving up on your pathway with spirit. You have your life to lead, and that is often hard.

So is the pathway of your spirit journey. There are periods of feast and periods of seeming famine. Many of you try too hard. This is probably the most common of all errors. Don't have any anxieties of what may or may not happen. Just get into your relaxed state of mind and allow what can happen to happen.

You have found out about spirit. Many go through their whole lives without knowing. Don't give up on it, ever. If you need to because of the burden of life okay, but don't give up, put it on one side to be picked up later. You are on your journey, and the next step will always be there waiting for you.

As with pieces of evidence, the greater path of mediumship needs your strength to carry on. Don't give up on spirit, they will never give up on you.

One other point. You can never go backwards you will always keep the progress you have made so far.

Try to see your steps

We usually progress in small steps and sometimes they are not easy to identify. Almost every time you sit in circle or even if you are more advanced, every demonstration you do there will be a step forward. It may be something you feel is insignificant but it will always be there and it will be used again in the future.

When we are not conscious of our steps, we may think that we are stagnant but if you look at every little link you do in practice there will be something you can pick up on.

But it isn't always small steps. From time to time you will come across something you give that makes you think, 'wow' I've not done that before! Maybe you have jumped up a whole staircase, but if you look back closely you will see that all those little insignificant things are all part of this great leap. Very often too, new growth will reflect a hope that you have put to spirit, that you can work in a certain way.

Small, solid steps are the way to build a great storehouse of knowledge and ability. Try to recognise them as you go along.

Be an explorer!

I have spoken about exploring each persons' character and we have journeyed through their home.

Sometimes this is not where the best evidence is to be found. Often it is outside.

Start your exploration in the garden, mention everything you see and feel how significant each part is. Maybe they grew produce, it could be mainly flowers. Which types of veg or flowers are present? Which is the most liked or most important?

Try going further afield, where did he/she journey to? What is the scenery, is there a coast, mountains, rivers, lakes or forests? From this as you feel into whatever landscape is there, move around, some areas will represent memories and some will be a liking for a particular environment.

Check out any wildlife, it could have a special meaning.

I remember once seeing an owl in a tree and that was all I needed for the whole reading. Again, this is to emphasise how important it is to give the unusual information as soon as you see or hear it.

The importance of this is to harness your clairsentience with your vision and feel into all the places you see. Each will have a meaning.

Try healing mediumship

During your development please spare some time to investigate the power of healing. Once you can link with spirit you can all do it, but it is most suited to those who blend well with passive mediumship. This does not mean you have to be a passive person!

Healing is a very profound type of mediumship but is often overlooked.

Give it a try.

Re-set your intention

When you decide to try healing mediumship it is wise to prepare a clean slate and re-set your intention. Healing is a passive form of mediumship and differs greatly from mentally active mediumship, so try to connect with spirit more deeply and in an atmosphere of peace and calm.

Ask a healing guide to step forward and give you a sign that they are there. A sign so you will recognise them in the future. Ask for the highest and the best available.

Your intention should be to provide the best solution to the problem. Ask for the best result and leave the rest to spirit. In healing, you are just the petitioner who sets the project in motion. If your patient is present you may be conscious of acting as a conduit of the power from spirit to your patient.

Your intention should always be goodwill to all.

Healing mediumship tends to attract those with a great sense of care and compassion, which forms a great basis for the healing angels to work with. Finding a healing group and having healing qualifications is very important. When you qualify you will have insurance to cover any healing you may do in person.

Feel into healing energies

The energies used in healing are very different from what we have discussed so far. They are deeper, which represents the greater connection with spirit. They manifest in many ways, most often heat and coolness. As you feel into these energies you will become aware of power. This attunement to power will be much different to your attunement for your usual work with spirit which uses vibration or frequency.

If you choose to develop as a healing medium you will start to be aware of many different energies. This makes complete sense. Each and every patient has different needs and therefore the energies required will be different for each one.

There is also the fact that the patient may need a certain specialist and so there will often be a specialist guide in attendance who will have a different energy to your regular guide. Sometimes you will be conscious of this, sometimes not.

Be aware of your healing progress

Healers tend to be less concerned about their own progress as they focus on just allowing things to happen, but in all forms of mediumship progress will be there, and as a healer you will want to be the best channel you can be just as with the rest of your work.

It is not easy to check your progress as a healer as you will be more reliant on feedback than usual, but you can gather information from what your patients feel. Keep records of how each regular patient progresses to help with this.

Don't be surprised that as you develop as a healer that your consciousness of the power becomes less. This is because you are more and more in tune with spirit and the difference is therefore less. There is no good way to explain this clearly except to say that sometimes less is more. It is often the case that as you feel less your patient feels more as you become a better and better channel for the power.

Two things to note here are that as you are working so closely with spirit during healing your mediumship will improve, and secondly that if you have found progress slow in active mediumship you may suddenly blossom when working with healing as you are more suited to passive mediumship. If this happens to you then you have found your first niche.

Don't use your own energy

Remember, when healing that you are just a channel for the healing energies. This is very important. Your compassion can lead you to be so giving that you drain yourself of your own natural life energy. What is more is that you can drain all those around you too! I know, I have done this and I got a telling off from spirit. If you trust spirit then let them do it. We only have to ask once, sincerely, and leave it to our guides.

As well as healing as the channel we can also work when the patient is not present. This is called absent healing and works just as well, sometimes better. The process is as follows. Healing medium asks spirit. Spirit receives and goes as directed. Power then goes to the patient.

Be confident in a job well done. Spirit healing never fails, the power will always go to the whole situation and spread wellbeing to those who are worrying about your patient as well as the patient themselves.

Prepare to be an all-day everyday medium

This really applies to healing. When going about your daily life you will notice people in need or in pain. As a healing medium you can offer up a short prayer asking for them to be supported or healed in the confidence that your link with spirit is there and help will arrive. You will most likely get an acknowledgement of your prayer from spirit. Perhaps by a coolness or a tingling sensation.

So, you can be a healing medium all day. There is no limit to this no matter how many people in need you see there will always be someone in spirit waiting to help.

With regard to other forms of mediumship, you may get information for someone in the supermarket queue. This does not mean that you can impose yourself on the other poor customer. They will come to spirit in their own way if they wish.

Many people of other faiths could be either angry or distraught if you took this action. Furthermore, spirit people are not dumb they know the problems of working this way. If you believe you are getting information in this sort of situation examine it. The chances are that you are working with a psychic energy and not with mediumship at all.

Set your focus

Set your focus for every session, workshop, course or demonstration. This is important to keep you on track and avoid development of wishy-washy techniques, which in turn lead to wishy-washy practices and poor results.

Try to focus on expanding different aspects of evidence. This will bring a fullness and richness to your mediumship which enables you to serve the needs of spirit in giving what they want to give in the way they want it. In the end we are working for spirit and the sitter too in the best way we can. We are not here to serve our own self-esteem. Feel pleased about a job well done of course, but remember, our focus is on those we are serving in this world and the next.

Maintain your focus too

When you have decided your strategy don't jump around from one thing to another. Be patient. Soon after realising that yes, you have the potential to become a medium you will choose an area you would like work in. This could be in giving one to one sittings, providing spirit art, or undertaking public demonstrations; the list is endless. You will also have found your preferred and strongest method of receiving information. You now have to decide how and where. Opportunities always arise.

I believe that the best way forward is to follow the path of least resistance. Keep a focus on what you do well and the rest will follow. If you are lucky enough to see clearly work on that and let other skills develop in due course. Don't rule anything out by saying things such as 'I never get names,' if you feel that you will never receive them as you are blocking out that aspect.

The focus on your type of work is important too. If you would like to give private readings take every opportunity you can to do so, in circle, and maybe with trusted friends who don't mind if you are not the finished article.

There is a natural progression once you start doing this which you can take as far as you like or stop when you want. Remember, you are in control.

You may be asked to work at a church reading day or psychic tea. You will not have been asked out of the blue. Someone somewhere has shown confidence in you. Take the opportunity.

You will prove yourself capable and will probably be invited to give a public service or a demonstration. Make sure that you are ready. Before accepting this you should have worked with an experienced medium on the platform and developed to the stage where you have given more than half of the messages, and, in the case of accepting to give a church service you will already have given the address in a service on more than one occasion. If you fulfil these requirements by all means accept any offer. Your tutor should already have suggested that you are ready, if not have a chat with her/him to find out their honest opinion.

Don't jump from one thing to another but allow a natural progression to take place.

Don't question your sitter

The job of the medium is to give information not seek it from your sitter. If you really need to ask a question, ask spirit, although truly the way to go about this is not to question at all but feel into the information.

If you see something as routine as a football, don't ask your sitter if they played football or their family did. Ask your link why is the football significant? And first of all just say to your sitter 'I am seeing a football, let me find out why.'

Asking questions is one of the most common bad habits a medium can get into. It shows a lack of trust in spirit which will never be cured whilst the questions keep being asked. There are ways to train yourself to pull away from this. It is a matter of how you present the information you have. Let me give you an example.

'Can you tell me why I am seeing a fish?

Or;

'You would understand why I am seeing a fish.'

This is a change in grammar and emphasis. In the second example you are confident that what spirit are giving is true. It really doesn't matter if you, the medium doesn't know the meaning as long as the sitter does.

Be conscious of your approach to spirit

Approach those in your spirit team with reverence. Try to appreciate that they have had to move much further towards you than you have towards them. They are doing most of the hard work. Your guides will have spent many years in training to be strong enough to work with you. Give them due credit.

Just as you are trying to be an agent of the divine, understand that they have already achieved this. So, approach your spirit team not with brashness or arrogance, but with an attitude of quiet confidence and respect. This will bring about a much stronger rapport which will be reflected in your progress.

Review your targets

Remember that in the beginning we spoke about having a focus and finding your place in your work with spirit. Once you have been working in group for a while you will want to settle your ambitions in some form. Setting a target or targets is a good way of bringing control to your development so you are not overloaded with lots of varying pathways. You have your whole life to explore many things and they will come forward at the correct time.

By this time you will have a good idea where you want to be. Put a time scale in place too, but don't worry too much if it slips a little, life gets in the way sometimes. This is a good time too to look at your earlier ambitions, are they now much greater? I hope so, it is so easy in the early stages to believe that giving short readings to a friend will be enough but as you start this you will realise that there is a great need in the world for reassurance and comfort. Look now for how you can be a real benefit to mankind.

Be easy on yourself

We all tend to analyse our performance in a negative and dwell on what we missed rather than think about what we succeeded in doing. We worry too about our standard and the consistency of the information we give.

Be aware that we will not always blend so easily with one person as another. We don't do this in our normal life and so why would it be that we should blend equally well with all in spirit. It just isn't the case. As time goes by we come to identify these differences and are able to use them to describe the nature of the person we have in spirit.

Your guides will help you as much as they can with this. They use your life experiences a great deal to help pass on information so it is more difficult if someone comes through with whom you have little in common.

It is so easy to be hard on yourself when you are keen to do your best, however, practice makes perfect and the more you work the better you will become.

Be patient, don't expect too much too soon and also think that what you have given may be very important to your sitter although you thought it was not much. This will happen quite a lot over the years.

Practice sitting with spirit

Try sitting in the quiet, relax and focus just on your breath. Let any thoughts drift away as you relax your mind and body with each breath.

Once you are relaxed just imagine your mind to become open. At first just a little and then more so. This will bring about a feeling of calm and is the time to invite your guide to come close. Ask them to give a sign that they are there. Each guide will always give their own sign but at the moment ask for, and focus on the one who is helping you with mediumship. The sign could be anything but is usually a tingling sensation or a touch, but can often be a pressure, a fragrance, or even an itch. You might have to ask for this several times so don't worry if you sense nothing to start with. Just ask for them to bring it more strongly.

As you regularly sit in the presence of spirit you will feel a sense of peace and contentment which will gradually expand into your whole life. The blending of your two energies together is a magical thing show your love and trust of spirit as they bring theirs to you. This attunement to those who work with you is the lynch pin of all your developing mediumship. Nothing can be achieved without contact and when sitting in the power you are creating an opportunity for the blending to grow. Sometimes the emotions in this blending of souls can be quite overwhelming.

Imagine too, the feeling of joy from your guides when you first make contact with them. They too are blessed as for most, although they will be helping, will not be able to reach their wards on earth.

Think of this attunement as a telephone exchange or a communications satellite. It has to be built before it can work, but then huge quantities of communications can be made. The more you sit in peace with your guides the better your communications will become.

Practice one to one sittings

Mainly you will be doing this in your group, but of course this will continue throughout your development and into the public arena. Some of you may only have family or friends to practice with but this is ok. A common argument is that you run out of contacts but that is a fallacy. Just think of how many people you have met since childhood, through school, work and extended family. The list runs into thousands and any one of them can come through and want to speak to you.

When giving readings don't go too deep, retain an active mind and allow things to happen. The moment we stop allowing, we start to think, and this is not helpful and your quality will drop. You will know when this happens as you will lose your link with spirit. Restart the process and rejoin spirit. What happens otherwise is that you drop into the psychic faculty. You will feel your mind move from spirit and go forward to your sitter.

Throughout your development period and onward to the platform you will be involved in one to one communication. It is good practice to master this before attempting any public work.

Soul development

One theme of mediumship which runs constantly alongside all the others is the development of the soul. Not just our own but also those we come into contact with. The knowledge we gain along the way brings with it a responsibility for the way we act, for what we give in information and also a responsibility to help those who come to us in need. Examine our fifth principle of Personal Responsibility. No-one else is going to take that away from us. We must handle it ourselves and therefore take great care in what we do both inside and outside working with spirit. Many people will set you on a pedestal and many others try to knock you off it. Don't give them any opportunity.

Our purpose is to bring comfort and healing of mind, body and soul; to banish fear from the lives of those who come to us, thus allowing the pathway of their lives to progress as it should.

We bring balance and understanding as well as learning. Very often what we bring most is hope. All these things help the eternal progress and development of the souls of others, not forgetting ourselves, as we embark on a life of service.

Never forget the divine link

Whatever your form of mediumship be confident in that you are opening a link to the divine, nothing less. Awesome isn't it?

Remember we mentioned at the start that mediumship is not supernatural it is very much a natural thing. There have been mediums throughout history and always will be. Some have been the focus of various religions but the vast majority are unsung heroes.

If after reading the previous notes in this book you are still seeking fame and fortune you are in the wrong place and reading the wrong book.

A great part of mediumship is linking your consciousness with that of the spirit world, the universal consciousness. This link is a thing of beauty and will bring you great joy. Many people use the term 'Ambassador of Spirit' and this is true.

I like the term 'Agent of the Divine', it sounds a little more proactive and being active is spiritually very important for the progress of the human race.

Isn't it wonderful to be part of such a great movement?

Section 3: Transition

Go where your heart takes you

The world has a great need of mediums healers and teachers of spirit.

You have now taken steps to fill part of this need.

So many of our population are crying out for awareness and knowledge. Many people live in fear of the hereafter, many too wonder about the suffering of others. Some in grief are inconsolable. Our job is to fill those voids. To bring forward light and healing. To turn hope into knowledge and bring an understanding that life goes on, that there need be no fear; that we all live our lives and every moment we live contributes to the growth of our souls. This is our purpose. A great and noble purpose. As you move towards working in public, think about what part you want to play in this great movement of enlightenment.

Don't be satisfied with the psychic faculty, develop your mediumship. Be the best medium you can be. Strive for perfection but understand that the best you can be will fall short of this aim.

The most difficult part of your transition from private to public demonstrating is confidence in yourself. You should already have developed confidence in your spirit team. Once you have full trust in your team the rest will develop through experience.

It is important at this time that you continue in your circle. That way each time you work in public with your tutor or mentor you can return to circle and analyse where you can improve, think about what you missed, but most of all, accept where you did well and build upon that strength.

This is a very exciting or perhaps even nerve-wracking phase of your progress. Learning to work out there in public. Be excited and enjoy the nervous anticipation. Remember spirit will always be with you throughout and never more so than when you begin stepping out.

This stage in your progress is very variable. Some people get really empowered by the thought of their first public work, others can be in a state of dread. If you have practiced public speaking and perhaps spoken out loud an address or two   this will help you be confident.

At this point you should have a mentor, maybe your group leader, who will allow you to share a platform. Whoever you share with it is important that they are experienced enough to carry the whole demonstration if need be.

Don't give up on your destiny

As you start your transition from training to public work your greatest enemy is fear. We are all naturally cautious of beginning a new phase. Be confident in your preparation. All the time and effort you have put in counts for a lot. Your tutor will probably be the person who mentors you through your first demonstrations and services. They will take the larger share of the evening and gradually increase your part in the event as you gain experience.

Listen to, and indeed ask for their honest criticism of your work and also feel for the energy of those in the audience. They will know you are new and be sympathetic to your cause. The world loses many potential healers and mediums each year as those with the potential and developed abilities reach this stage and fall away. Don't be one of these people. The world needs you.

Consider your preparation. Have you rushed into the public domain too quickly? Lots of aspiring mediums are eager and jump into the public arena too soon. However, many more decide not to take that step which is a great pity as this is usually not through lack of ability but through a lack of preparation.

Once you have gone through all the previous stages you should know your potential and promise. Your tutor should already have told you that you are ready to work in various locations with support, leading to you going it alone.

Take up the challenge, move forward and start spreading joy, comfort and healing.

Stay humble

Sometimes, no matter how careful we are the enormity of what we do leads to an over inflated ego. Don't worry too much, if this happens there is usually someone around who will burst your bubble and bring you down to earth. If so, thank them, as they have done you a big favour. Remember we are just agents, not the divine light itself.

Why us? Well, why not? Although we must remain down to earth we have to accept that for whatever reason or by whatever chance we have an unusual, even abnormal ability.

When we realise the enormity of what we do, that we work with the universal consciousness it is hard to keep our feet on the ground. Consider actors and actresses thrust into stardom after years of hard work. How difficult it must be for them. Our load is not so hefty but it is easy to lose our way. We can't fulfil our role and carry our responsibility if we let our ego run away with us.

Remember your spirit buddy. Ask them to tell you if you are getting too big for your boots. Certainly, we should have a pride in what we do, so you see, we have a balance to achieve a steady movement forward. There will always be greater and lesser mediums than you. Respect one and support the other.

It helps to prevent being pompous if we remain in awesome wonder of spirit.

Stand tall

When you step up on the rostrum from the very first time stand tall. You may feel nervous inside, and if so gather yourself together and be proud to be there serving spirit. When you are speaking you are the one in charge and in control. You need to show this, as the more confident you appear the more confidence your audience will have in you. They will become interested, more receptive and want to be part of what's going on. If you stand tall and confident you will find that this stays with you and each subsequent event will ease your nerves until they go completely. We are agents of spirit and need to show that we are a part of something much greater.

Work to build your confidence

In the introduction to this section I spoke about confidence. Practice will help you with the confidence in your spirit team, but the self-confidence you will need for working publicly will only come through experience. There are lots of things that will help build your own esteem.

We have established that you will have confidence in your spirit team. That is essential. Secondly, you will need to have established confidence in the person who will be leading you on to the platform. This will be your circle leader or mentor and they will already have established their way of working and be confident in working publicly. Have confidence in them, and confidence in that they have confidence in you, otherwise they would not have invited you to work with them.

That only leaves yourself. Your preparation will be what carries you through. Wear something smart but comfortable. If you can walk into the venue and people say, 'oh you must be the medium', you have got it right. You are already earning their respect. Sit for a while before you leave home, just to relax. Allow yourself plenty of time.

When you are on the rostrum and your tutor asks if you have anything say yes. Their true question should be are you ready? This is because strictly speaking you should fully enter the power as you stand up and your first link will be there. In any event just say yes. Don't expect to be amazing your first time. If you are, well, that's fabulous but be happy that you have given your first one or two links.

After this first time your confidence will build up steadily.

Throw your voice

You might think what has throwing your voice got to do with mediumship. The answer is very little, but it is important when you demonstrate.

The old adage is 'The deaf ones always sit at the back'. This is not necessarily true but it is important when you work publicly that your information reaches everyone. Even if your recipient turns out to be on the front row, everyone is interested and want to be part of the service. If you speak quietly to someone at the front all those behind will lose interest and then you have lost your audience. So make sure you keep everyone engaged in your demonstration by being audible to them all and maintain eye contact too.

Compare yourself to other mediums

This is not a competition, but you can learn a lot from observing other mediums work the rostrum. Make a point, as you yourself are starting to work publicly, to see as many mediums work as you can. Observe the difference in those who have a great deal of experience and those who are perhaps just a few steps ahead of you.

Also, observe their style of delivery and note their level of confidence.

Look too at the type of information they give. Each one will have strengths in certain areas, some in many areas. You might well find something in their abilities which mirrors your own or things that you feel you could easily move into. There is no such thing as the complete medium but by observing others it will help you become more and more rounded in your own mediumship.

Look which mediums command the room when they are demonstrating, check out their dress code, feel how they blend with the congregation and what levels of control they have. All of these skills influence the way you can become the complete medium.

Don't compare yourself to other mediums

What?

Yes, I know, I've just recommended that you do!

It is very easy to think that others are better than you. So many of us do this. The reason, I think, is that whilst we see the reaction of sitters to other mediums and are impressed, we tend to undervalue our own contribution.

Your journey is not about them, it is about you. You are unique, embrace this fact, and understand that you will develop in your own way.

If you look at other mediums and think they are better than you, you will eventually believe it. The opposite can also happen that you judge other mediums as not being capable. If on the other hand you view others as being inferior to you then you are feeding a part of your ego you can best be without.

All mediums have their own struggles and due to us all having heightened sensitivity we are all vulnerable. Try to observe others in a way that will help you, not by comparing with yourself but the way they get information and sometimes the way they don't when they should.

Sometimes you will witness others working in a way you would rather avoid. That's good, it gives you a positive outlook, but just don't work in the way they do.

Send a positive thought of thanks for the lesson and try to send good wishes and help to those mediums who you feel are not serving spirit or their sitters.

Overall compare yourself to others where you can receive help towards your goals and use any exhibition of poor mediumship as a way to avoid poor work. There is always a positive outcome if you learn the lessons of both good and bad.

Embrace any failures

Not everything is a part of an easy straight path. There will be times when you don't manage to pass on all that you receive. There will be times too when you leave your recipient needing more, and others when your spirit contact hasn't made themselves known unequivocally. This is caused by, for whatever reason, we have not been able to blend with our spirit contact as well as we should. We cannot be in tune with everyone. You were the best pathway available at the time, so although we feel a certain lack of success on these occasions, it may be that your sitter came very rarely to church and spirit took the best opportunity available. Don't dwell on it, allow it to be part of your experience and use it to grow. There are other areas which show more of a weakness than a failure and many of these can be rectified quite easily.

You could for example have a weakness in prayer or giving your address. These can be worked on at home or in circle. A good tip is 'keep prayers short and make addresses long.'

Give due consideration to weak areas or events and work with your team to fill the gaps.

Remember no-one is perfect, but don't let that stop you trying!

Nurture your ego

As you go through the transition from trainee to medium it is important you maintain a level of self-worth. Neither build yourself up as a public figure but maintain a confidence in your value as a medium. You need to keep a level of ego to remain strong but if you allow your new found confidence to run amok it could bring your downfall.

If you lose track of this there will be extravagant claims made and you may find yourself telling fortunes which will not come true. It's just another trip to la la land. It will take a long time bring yourself back to working well.

Sadly, I have known several mediums take this path where the pursuit of money is more important than the pursuit of truth. Keep your ego in check, both expanding and withering. Like so many aspects of mediumship this is about balance.

Keep on studying

You may think that now that you are working under supervision and in public that you don't need to practice so much.

That would be a nice relief but sadly it's not true. This period will be very busy. You will still need to practice with your group to help refine your skills but also reflect on all the public work you do too. It's good to compare what you are able to give in public with what your abilities are in circle. Often when you work on the rostrum you receive more information than before. You are in an empowered situation and therefore you are able to move into that power and do more. There will be many people you have not met before and their situation will be unique, so you may find that your links in spirit are working to help in areas unknown to you.

 Once you receive information a new way or a different kind of information you can practice it in your circle. This way your existing learning is blending with your new learning from public work.

Don't forget to carry on reading. Lots of books by mediums describe their time in transition, the obstacles they met and overcame. They can be very helpful to you.

The transition is an exciting time. A time of great personal growth, so maintain your studies and use your experience to help those in your group who are going to go through it in future.

It's not about me

When we are going through this change it can be all consuming. Try not to allow this to happen. It's not about us, it is about spirit and your sitter. We can end up thinking about where we are and what is happening almost all the time and this leads us astray.

This can lead to us talking about ourselves and our journey when we should be giving a spiritual address. We should be aiming for an inspired speech from spirit, your audience deserves this, not a monologue about your day shopping. (Don't laugh, I have witnessed this and worse). Similarly, don't talk about yourself and your memories during a message. You may have a similar memory to your sitter but you need to relay their experience back to them not tell them yours.

Be gentle

In the course of our mediumship we will be giving many messages of comfort to those who are in a difficult place. We have a duty of care to those who are vulnerable, a duty to be gentle. To present the truth in an easy manner.

There are many things that happen on earth that leave regrets and a need for reconciliation. There, of course, will be many times too where our clients have suffered a great loss. Many who don't have our knowledge and understanding that no-one ever dies.

We have a chance to bring sunshine to many grieving souls through truth and enlightenment.

There are times too when we help those who have passed. Many people take their own lives and need to give an explanation to those left behind. We can help remove guilt from all parties and bring understanding.

All these things need to be carried out in a gentle manner.

We should always be thankful for the great honour we have in bringing comfort to these situations

Remove the fear

Removing the fear from the lives of many is another role of the medium. Many people live their lives in fear of death. Some that it will be the end of everything and so fear they will not leave a legacy. Others that they will not have lived their lives sufficiently well to earn a place away from hell and damnation.

We can help such people by bringing evidence, and hopefully enough evidence to prove that there is no death, but is this enough?

This body of evidence has to be very good quality to take away an emotion that many have held for all their lives. If you imagine you are on a jury and the defendant faces a huge jail term what level of evidence would you need to vote for a conviction? This is the level we should try to achieve during our sittings, to prove beyond reasonable doubt, that our loved ones have passed on safely. This is quite a responsibility.

We also have an opportunity to spark an interest in an area that they may well have entered reluctantly, and come to us as a last chance, the least likely option to find peace.

Our job as 'agents of the divine' is not just to bring the comfort we so often do but to have the people we meet leave with questions.

Questions such as, ` Why did I not know of this? How is it done? Why is this not taught to children? And hopefully 'Can I do this too'

A great many people we meet would love to have the knowledge we have in order to share comfort and take away fear. We represent the opportunity they need to have a fear free life and be able to pass this on to many others

The removal of fear is one of our greatest responsibilities but also one of the best opportunities to bring spiritual awareness into many lives.

Accept those who don't believe

Don't let the naysayers get you down. Accept that their pathway is not to link with spirit.

The burden of proof is on us. This is why we have to be the best we can. For most of us it's not easy and there are many who scoff. (Hands up all of you who scoffed at all things spiritual in the past.) Yes, my hand went up too.

Many will invent all sorts of unlikely explanations for what we do, mind-reading, cold reading, madness, alien intervention, anything unlikely, anything except the simple truth; for it is simple. The problem is the natural and simple truth of what we do has been pushed aside for thousands of years by those seeking power.

This inbuilt scepticism is actually a positive thing for those of us who take this path. Do we seek blind faith in what we believe and do? No, we have suffered that for many generations. The scepticism of others forces us to be on our metal, to do what we do well and this extends our individual and communal abilities.

We have to accept that for many the truth is difficult to accept. It is not our job to push our knowledge on to others. We lay the truth in front of them for them to pick up as they will. When and if the time is right for them they will take up our thirst for knowledge.

So, we accept those who don't believe, wish them well and let them go. They don't share our path.

Embrace change

Embrace the changes that being a working medium brings.

Working correctly with spirit brings great contentment which will change your attitude to life.

Embrace the changes within your work as a medium, it will constantly evolve and develop in unexpected ways if you allow it to.

You will become more sensitive to others, especially their needs. Your compassion will grow and you will be more sensitive in yourself. Don't allow this to make you vulnerable but treat it as a strength and one that can be controlled. Don't be weighed down by the needs of others, ask for healing and put their woes to the world of spirit.

Why does this change of sensitivity come about? I believe it is because you are now in a position to help others through your link with the universal consciousness. This is especially so in healing mediumship.

Another change you will be happy to embrace is the process of greater communion with spirit leading to greater abilities. Working with spirit does not mean that your life's challenges are over, far from it, but your greater understanding will allow you to place them as necessary experiences and put them into perspective within the greater scheme of things.

So embrace change!

Stay dissatisfied

This may sound a strange tip, possibly a negative one, but having an essence of dissatisfaction is good. While you are dissatisfied you will not stagnate. You will constantly seek betterment. So, this is a good thing, how are we to move forward otherwise?

There are so many ways to improve your mediumship, look to be the best you can in everything you give and then start on the areas that you currently just touch upon.

Most contacts you link with in spirit have lived full lives here on earth. How can you possibly fit a whole life into a few minutes? The whole history of your contact is available to you, allow yourself to be moved into what part of their lives they want to talk about.

Don't be satisfied staying in your comfort zone and put a limit on their expression, go with the flow of your spirit contact. This will fill an area of dissatisfaction and let you start on another. Onwards and upwards. Don't stagnate.

Have courage

You have already shown courage by your first visit to the church, starting your awareness and development circles and stepping up to start working in public. So, courage is nothing new to you. In fact, this tip could have come at any time from Tip 1 to Tip 101.

I have chosen to include it here as you step forward to perform for the first time in public. This is where you have to show confidence in yourself as well as in spirit. You have developed the courage to speak out in circle and although there is no difference technically of course a little bit of nervousness will have to be overcome. You have shown the courage to fail as you have been training, now, do you have the courage to succeed?

We seek a life of service not success or fame, but we also need to succeed in our mediumship to the best of our ability.

Having read the biographies of many great mediums, they never sought fame, only an understanding of their gifts and the ability to serve. You don't need to be the best but just the best version of you. Have the courage to be this.

Enjoy being nervous

Yes, enjoy it! Your nerves bring your mind into the active state needed to demonstrate in public and being nervous is natural.

Why is it that we are nervous? Generally, we are stepping out into the unknown. We often wonder if anything will happen at all. Have confidence and trust your spirit team, you will never be left alone and also when you start your team will be especially close in order to help you move forward. I am sure that in the early stages they organise strong characters to come forward to be your links to spirit.

Of course, as you gain more and more experience this nervousness will settle down but you can still use it as a tool to stimulate your mind. When the level of nervousness starts to subside we can really enjoy our work. Usually as we start to speak to our audience the nerves diminish straight away.

Control the audience

When you step on to the rostrum, especially in a demonstration assume control. You are the focus of the evening. It is your responsibility (with the chairperson) to ensure everything runs smoothly.

Maintain eye contact throughout as this keeps peoples' interest. When you engage the whole audience, you may see people nodding as if the message was for them, they have become involved. Your job is to keep them all involved throughout, by your speech, gestures and evidence.

You may have to deal with various situations that develop during your demonstrations. As a side note I was demonstrating in the middle of a divine service when a drunk came in demanding money, threatening to burn the church down. Fortunately, I had a very good chairperson on that occasion, but was prepared to deal with it myself. So be aware that things may happen and take them in your stride.

If you find things are happening you cannot deal with, stop and ask the chair to deal with it. That part is their responsibility. You will be able to deal with most things yourself, for example if someone has a fit of coughing, offer them water, the chair or stewards will supply this. Should people start talking as you are working just catch their eye and ask if they can take some of the evidence too, or just ask if they are all right. This is normally good enough to make them be quiet. You will find your own ways of keeping control.

Review your early public encounters

After your first few demonstrations don't be overly critical of yourself. Of course, there will be some things which were less than perfect but you are not yet the finished article. The places you are working will be made aware that at this stage you are still a trainee and whoever you are sharing the platform with will be supportive of you. If you find that you have missed something don't worry, you won't miss it next time. Be thankful for the lesson.

The sincere medium will always want to improve and question whether they are good enough. At this stage you are a trainee and perhaps not quite at the standard you want to set yet, but the more conscious you are of the small errors you might slip into the better placed you are to put them right.

In this way you can turn a weak area into a position of strength.

Never lose your sense of wonder

Never cease to be amazed by your link with spirit. The fact that you can be a messenger between the two worlds is magical. Even when you have worked thousands of times it is still a magical experience both for you and those who witness your work. For some it may be their first introduction to spirit and you can share their emotion.

Hang on to your wonder and respect the divine, the Great White Light, the Universal Consciousness. Respect, too, your spirit team, the agents who work with you as part of your journey. Be thankful for the gift placed upon you and the ability to pass it on.

Section 4: You, The New Medium

Make a difference

Am I worthy? This is a question often asked when we realise the enormity of what we do. You have got this far and another bold step beckons. By now you are well aware of spirit being with you. You have developed trust in your team and you are providing evidence during practice. The answer is, 'Of course you are worthy!' How much effort have you put in to achieve what you have? This doesn't count for nothing.

Seek out the uniqueness of your contact. They are just as unique as you are. Names are rarely unique…. personality and experiences are, so your blending with the link from spirit should allow you to give every single essence of their being.

Finally, it's your turn, be confident!

It is your first solo public demonstration. Remember you are in command.

You have been pushed, cajoled, entreated or otherwise persuaded to take your step onto the rostrum to give mediumship.

How do you feel? Most likely rather nervous, maybe inspired or excited, possibly in abject fear but this is the culmination of your efforts over previous months and years. Now is the most challenging step.

You are on your own. Or are you? By this time there should be no doubt that your team will be with you. Be confident. Don't expect to give the best evidence ever, just know that spirit will be with you. That they have prepared for this moment too. Go through your routine and step into your power as you mount the rostrum.

Smile, for you are about to touch souls.

Relax after your demonstration

Some people are more nervous after they have demonstrated than before. Take some time out, have a cup of tea. Chat with the person who chaired for you. Others may well approach with congratulations.

There is often one person who is not happy with the demonstration. That person is you. Don't be too self-critical, give yourself an honest assessment. Yes, you will probably have missed things but nobody else knows that. Your demonstration is over. You cannot go back. What you can do is appraise the many pieces of information you gave. Perhaps you could have delivered them a little better, but perhaps not. There is always room for improvement. That will never stop, so don't worry about that. It has to be that way.

Look forward to your future events with eagerness. Another opportunity to serve and another opportunity for growth.

Try to fulfil the burden of proof

Now you are working fully on your own you have to carry the burden of proof, your mentor has stepped aside, hopefully to help another. Remember your journey from your first circle as you found you were able to supply relevant information. Remember too the way you have developed this and the many ways you now receive evidence.

Each and every skill you have developed can be used by spirit to prove themselves alive after so-called death. Each will use a different blend of your skills, which shows how useful your training has been.

At the start the level of information expected of you was quite small. I remember being excited at giving just a couple of correct pieces. So now the level of expectation has increased as you have travelled through awareness, development, and practised platform with an experienced medium.

You will be using all your skills to give a level of evidence which constitutes proof. You cannot always do this. It depends on your ability to blend with the information that each spirit person wants to give you. There is another reason too which is more subjective. Maybe the need of the sitter is to come to your church or group more than just once. Perhaps they need to build up more slowly and receive pieces if information from several mediums to build up a level of confidence. Perhaps spirit know the needs of the sitter include being in a friendly spiritual environment. Remember that we serve the needs of the spirit and the sitter both, and we will not know either. All we can do is pass on the information we receive without changing it.

When you passed from awareness and through your time in development you accumulated many skills. Every link that comes to you will use some of those but not others. This is why your tutor will have spent many hours focusing perhaps on time slices through the lives of those in spirit and at other times their occupation, family, hobbies etc. Some of these aspects will be important to some and absent in others.

This is what makes our job interesting, every time we serve a church or do a demonstration it will be different, all our skills will come into play at some point and new skills will emerge. All for the purpose of proving eternal life.

Once we have given evidence to a sitter and are confident that we have accurately given a level of evidence to prove this we can be happy that we have given a good reading.

Think about your continuous professional development

We know that we can never achieve perfection and that knowledge in itself leads to the belief that continuous improvement is possible. Some of the methods to keep developing are quite simple. For example, never stop sitting with spirit, in groups or just you and your team. This is so important.

The more you sit with your guides the greater the blending between you and spirit becomes. This enables new ways of working to develop naturally. It also helps develop those areas you are already competent in. Sitting is essential if you hope to go on to work with inspiration or if you want to pursue working in altered states.

If you can continue to sit in circle you can sent out thoughts to be challenged in new areas. Be prepared to have to wait for further success. Learn to enjoy getting a negative response so you can investigate what you receive to find the truth. Spirit are never wrong, so investigate your 'noes'. Circles are a great way to practice this.

If you can, find a group with several other mediums who are working. This enables an exchange of views and talents to take place in an atmosphere of mutual learning. Others may be suffering the same issues as you or may have overcome them, so giving you an insight as to how to proceed.

This does not mean you should quit your development group. As you have progressed you have the chance to be a contributor to the development of the others. It may also give you a chance to lead the circle from time to time.

Always work with kindness in your heart

If there is one thing to be as a medium it is to be kind.

There will be many difficult messages you will have to put across. There are rare times when you have to filter the messages. There are so many difficult situations, murder victims, suicides and passings where family disputes have not been settled.

Keep your mind on what our purpose is. To serve the needs of both spirit and the loved one remaining. We have to get spirits message across but do so in a kind manner with consideration and due care.

Take another example of a man in spirit who has spent many years in jail. Do we really want to voice this in public to his grieving daughter? Approach situations like this with extreme care. You will need to provide evidence but also avoid distressing the recipient further.

If your recipient is ever in distress, don't just charge on because you are on a run of giving your best evidence ever. Reign yourself in and ask the sitter if they want you to continue. In any event, at that point search for gentler evidence. Whatever the situation be kind and gentle. The balance of evidence and kindness is another responsibility we carry.

Section 5: Building Your Philosophical Talks

Today is full of possibilities

During writing this book I have been tempted to include a tutorial on the philosophical address. This is a very important part of the Spiritualist service and many mediums feel daunted by what is actually the easiest part of the service.

The reason for this is that you can draw on your life's experience to talk to others. Everything you see or touch can be brought into your philosophy or in fact can be the base from which you start.

Within your group set time aside to talk about spirit. Your hopes, dreams and experience. Share what you have read and discuss whether it feels right to you or not. Try to take on board the views of everyone else and their experiences too. As you attend your circles, demonstrations or services try to understand where the thoughts of each speaker are coming from and how they feel about spirit.

When learning to give an address start by thinking about the attributes of everyday things. At random, looking around as I write I see a hat, a folder, a multi socket and a candle holder and a diary. It is possible to build a story around each and every object.

Let's choose the hat to start with. How should we speak about it? So here goes, '*I have here a hat and this hat is designed to keep the sun off, so this represents protection. It is also the correct size for me and to a certain extent then is tailored for my needs. It also has a motif showing a love of sport, and therefore is linked to part of what makes me tick. There are many different types of hat and they can bring back many memories. Who can forget the fez of Tommy Cooper or the Fedora of Humphrey Bogart in 'Casablanca'?*

So, a simple hat can show our character and interests.

When we think of linking a hat to the world of spirit the protection of the hat represents the protection and guidance we receive from those who have gone before, a shield against those who would do us harm. It is a tailored to our needs and is therefore unlike any other as of course our needs are unique. The character of the hat shows the individuality we all have, and in some way expresses that to those we meet. Our character of course reflects all the good and bad things we have gone through and enjoyed or overcome in due measure. A hat also brings a measure of warmth and comfort which when we work with spirit we are conscious of, but it also applies to every single human being wherever they may be. Part of our job as spiritualists is to spread the warmth of this knowledge to those who live a life of drudgery or fear. To uplift that portion of humankind we come into contact with. Not just humankind though, this also applies to the animal kingdom, and those of you who have pets will know exactly what I mean.

In summary, where would we all be without that help and guidance from those in spirit?

That is a very short example, off the cuff, of what you can do to start developing speech when in circle. That example was not inspired. Just coming from ordinary thoughts but the more you can practice speaking out loud the more opportunity you are giving your guides to bring in the occasional word of inspiration on your way to giving a directly inspired full speech.

As well as objects I find that songs are a great source of inspiration. If I am travelling to a demonstration I sometimes turn on the car radio, it is amazing how often that the first song I hear is the source of my address or contains details about my first link.

Some suggestions of songs to compose a short address from. Each one can link to one of the seven principles shown later in the book. The principles are the basis of Spiritualist philosophy. Play these songs to yourself and write a short speech on each one. You will probably surprise yourself, especially if you sit in the power first and ask your guides to come close.

My Way by Frank Sinatra. You can link this to the principle of Personal Responsibility.

I Will Survive by Gloria Gaynor. You could tie this up to Eternal Progress.

Angels by Robbie Williams. This would link to 'The communion of spirit and the ministry of angels'.

Everybody Hurts by R.E.M. I would link this with the general philosophy of development through hardship.

Bittersweet Symphony. The Verve. I have given this off the platform. It would have been similar to how it set out below but with inspired parts throughout, and these would change in accordance with the needs of the audience. A good philosophy will be meaningful to all present.

My address would be something like this;

'Good evening everyone. Can anyone else remember the 1990's? Good. It's not just me then! Sadly, I was old enough to have a son who was into music at that time. Anyway, at that time in the late nineties there was a popular band that went by the name of 'Verve', maybe 'The Verve'. They produced a very popular album called Urban Hymns.

This is an interesting title as I am speaking about them in a church setting. Within this album is a song called Bittersweet Symphony which is the theme I want to speak about tonight.

The first line is 'It's a bittersweet symphony this life.'

There have probably never been truer words spoken.

None of us seem to have life easy. Let's check. How many of you have had an easy life? Just as I thought. Why would that be? Surely it can't be by chance that no-one has an easy life.

Of course, there are always good times within our lives and many joys. Let's take a few moments to think about the purpose of our lives. We know that we originated from spirit and that we all return, so why bother. What tempted us to spend this time on earth? Surely, we didn't just come down here for a holiday? I believe the answer to this is in the principle of eternal progress. I also believe that we came down here to enjoy or endure the whole gamut of human emotions, to understand the nature of having a physical body and the restrictions that places on our spiritual expression. In short to take another step in the progress of our souls' development.

So let us look back upon our lives, and consider what has helped us grow the most. This will almost always be the times when we have overcome strife of one kind or another, but there are times in our lives when perhaps through work or sports that we have learnt to be part of a team. A group growth if you will which brings a different dynamic to our personal growth. We are part of something greater.

This shows that although our lives are just a speck in the path of eternity, they are a vital part of our overall development. I often think of the time it would take us to develop from our initial spark of existence to the point where we make a conscious decision to have a spell down here on earth. A hundred years, surely longer than that? A thousand, a million? We won't know until we return, maybe there is no time in spirit and it is a matter of preparation and we could visit here at any time in our progression. We will find this out in due course.

Whichever way we find out about our long term pathway, the relevance to the here and now, and our use of the bittersweet experience will help us on our way. We should remain positive throughout our lives as much as we can, for although we learn the most by overcoming adversity there is much to be said for the joys in life and what they bring. The friendships of childhood, our first social development through choice, the joys of achievement at school. Falling in love. The rigours, but also the great pride and joy of parenthood and the profound love without the rigours of further generations. The greater appreciation of beauty, the inner beauty of people and the beauty of the world around us as we mature. All these things are part of our progress and should be greatly valued. For those of us who follow a spiritual path there is nothing to compare with the love and compassion we share with those in spirit. How often do we feel sadness for those who remain unknowing of this, the greatest of all aspects of life?

Life truly is a bittersweet experience and the key to being at peace is to achieve the balance between the good and the bad.

And so, I am sure some of you are thinking what about the symphony? Where does that come in?

I'm sure that at some point most of you will have listened to the great symphonies of the likes of Beethoven or Tchaikovsky.

In all symphonies there are themes which are repeated at times throughout, usually one main theme and several lesser ones. I have found that this is reflected in our lives that certain things seem to happen from time to time. Maybe this is because we didn't react properly the first time but perhaps too, we overcame a problem and the next time it occurred we overcame it more easily, or perhaps in a different way. It could be that the main theme is the thing which was our priority when we decided to visit the earth plane, and that the lesser themes are other lessons for us to learn.

Whatever the reason may be, the outcome is that when we leave here we are all more accomplished than when we arrived. Our maturity allows us to teach those who follow us, our future generations that they will have an insight into the things we have achieved which will allow them to pursue their own issues.

This applies too to those we meet throughout our lives, that through sharing our various experiences we can help others along the way. I believe that one thing which separates us from other life is our ability to show compassion and thoughtfulness to those around us, although I recognise that this is not just a human trait and animals do the same too on occasion.

It is when we understand these repeated themes in our lives that we can offer the assistance to those who are going through similar situations. The blending of the greater and lesser themes in our lives do indeed form a unique symphony for each and every one of us.

When these themes reach their ultimate crescendo, understanding and compassion come together in a glorious maturity of the spirit.

This then is how we can build up an address which will hopefully apply to everyone present in a certain measure, that we touch all souls and hopefully inspire those in the congregation to investigate what mediumship and spiritualism are all about.

This came about by investigating the title and some of the lyrics of a song. Try to pick out some of your own favourite songs and see how after a while inspiration from spirit will develop your thoughts from what could be a two minute speech into an address which will inspire others as well as yourself.

There are many things which can inspire us all. They don't have to be items or songs but could be time spent by a river or walking in the countryside. When you feel the urge just allow your mind to be inspired and write down a basic theme. Before too long you will find that you can easily talk for a short while on just about anything and find a meaning in it. This will progress into a blending of themes which allows you to expand what you say and certain parts will touch certain people. Once again, just as in routine mediumship it is in allowing the influence of spirit which enables you to be at your best.

Your speeches are not just about content. There are techniques which can help you make an impact. It is good to pause after each point made to allow your listeners to absorb what you are saying. The length of this pause is important, too short and there is no impact, too long and people will become bored. Experience will teach you what is best for you, and the timings will not always be the same. It is always good to vary your cadence and speak more quickly at some times than others. Changing the volume at certain points is important too, although you must remember that the people furthest away have to hear everything you say. Use gestures to include everyone in the atmosphere of your speech and maintain eye contact throughout your address.

Finally, smile, you are serving the spirit what could be better.

Section 6: The Pathway Of The Soul

Shine like the whole universe is yours

So, we have come to the end, or rather, the true beginning of our journey. What is its purpose? Why do we do it? At this point we have spent several if not many years of our lives searching for our purpose.

It is often said that all mediumship is healing, certainly there will always be an element of healing in all messages. Healing mediumship by its very nature brings both physical and emotional healing.

However, in being a medium and a spiritualist brings a more profound benefit. Our purposes are many. To bring comfort to those suffering a loss. To take away fear of death. To let people know that they can communicate with their loved ones and never lose them.

I believe the most important role of the spiritual person and all mediums is to heal the pathway of the soul of others. The role to let everyone know that this earthly life is just a mere speck of their existence and that they will return to their beautiful home richer for the experience of life in the body.

We should therefore embark on this journey of mediumship with great enthusiasm and now we have become working mediums work also to fulfil the needs in the soul of others. Our lives are all about service, to our fellow man, all life on earth and the earth itself. We have become ambassadors of the spirit world. We need to use this role to help those who struggle. To help those in chains of religion and ideology, to let them realise that just to be is a joy. To embrace who they are and be comfortable with it.

The pathway of each soul is unique, who are we to judge?

As you move forward into this role you may well find that people from the past reintroduce themselves into your life as they become more aware of the link you have with spirit, similarly more and more people enter your life not consciously knowing what they are seeking but they know that you have the answer.

So, for a while, which may be short or a lifetime, the paths of your souls may run side by side each one learning. Life really is a joy.

Finally, please remember you are the person you are today, not 5 years past, a month, week or even a day ago. Look back at your progress and look forward to a wonderful unfoldment of life which will lead who knows where. Exciting isn't it?

Section 7: The Seven Principles Of Spiritualism

Everything has beauty

The Seven Principles of Spiritualism:
- [ ] The fatherhood of God.
- [ ] The brotherhood of Man.
- [ ] The communion of spirit and the ministry of angels.
- [ ] The continuous existence of the human soul.
- [ ] Personal responsibility.
- [ ] Compensation and retribution hereafter for all the good and evil deeds done on earth.
- [ ] Eternal progress open to every human soul.

These principles always used to be followed by the words 'with liberty of interpretation.'

These seem to be omitted now but I believe that we should interpret them according to our own level of understanding.

Some thoughts on the seven principles

The fatherhood of God has nothing to do with gender. It is in my opinion the act of the seed of the universal consciousness being placed within the individual is what constitutes fatherhood. We have to remember that this term was couched in the language of Victorian England. I like this coupled with the phrase 'mother earth' thus the seed in placed within us which is then nurtured by our lives on earth in the physical realm.

The brotherhood of man tells us of a shared heritage. We come from spirit, inhabit a body and then return home. During this time on earth we have a total interdependence with each other. Every single time we have an interaction with someone, even if it is just a glance, there is an aspect of learning. So, all of our experiences with our fellow man bring about personal growth, whether the experiences are good, bad, happy or sad. I believe that one of our purposes is to experience many things in order to have compassion for others who are experiencing bad times we may have gone through ourselves, and also developing an understanding for their actions. This also helps us to share the joy when others succeed, or have their own beautiful experience.

The communion of spirit and the ministry of angels is really what mediumship entails and is the principle which separates Spiritualism from most other religions. Communion is what we use in all the many aspects of mediumship, whether this is healing, the various forms of trance or the more common readings and demonstrations. These are the parts we see, hear and feel, but there is another aspect of guidance, upliftment and support through life which we are not conscious of. When we talk about ministry, it is important to understand the meaning of ministry in this sense. It is the act of service, and so we understand that whatever you believe angels to be, is that their agency brings about service to humankind as a whole and individuals too.

We believe too it is true that we continue after what is termed physical death and our work is to bring enough evidence forward of this the those who seek find truth without doubt. This raises the question too of how long we existed as an individual in spirit before we decided to come to earth.

Personal responsibility regards both thoughts and actions. No-one can take away our guilt or sins just as no-one can take praise for what we do. We alone are responsible and should act accordingly throughout our lives.

The principle of Compensation and Retribution relates to what happens next after we pass back to spirit, or return home to spirit. Yes, we receive compensation for our good deeds and here we must again consider the meaning of retribution. I like to think of the retri as re-try. We have an opportunity to do things right and put any errors we have made back on track. We are not sent to hell and damnation. That is a thing of the earth plane to reinforce the power of individuals and religions too.

The final principle is about eternal progress. Each of us can continue to develop and learn after returning to spirit but remember too that our lives here are part of this eternity and that we learn many things whilst on earth that we cannot learn in spirit, otherwise there would be no point in coming.

Acknowledgments

(In chronological order)

The Allen family, William, Audrey, Peter and Carol, for their many years of hospitality at the Long Eaton healing group, their guides Dr Heinrich von Bach, Professor Eric Stahl, healers in spirit.

Ron Rafferty, transfiguration medium and automatic writer who introduced me to the group.

The tutors at the Arthur Findlay College who have put up with me on numerous courses, especially Sandie Baker CSNU, Minister Colin Bates and Minister Bill Thompson.

A special mention for 'Openteh', spirit guide of Arline Doherty for his teaching, mentorship and patience over the last ten years.

My own spirit team, led by 'Monica', with 'Joseph' and 'Jeremiah' without whom my life would be very empty.

Front cover and section headings all produced by the wonderful Shelley Youell and are subject to copyright. I am very grateful to Shelley for providing them and grateful too for the endorsement of such a great spirit artist and fellow medium.

No words can express my gratitude for these people and the many others who have brought me along this pathway. I am truly blessed.